Strengthening the new
Christian

Consolidating new believers
Aluízio A. Silva

The Vine U.S.A.
Richard Lee Spinos Translator/Editor

PREFACE

This book was originally prepared to be a teaching resource for small group leaders of The Vine International, a cell based group that began in southern Florida in 2009. It was designed to serve as a training manual for new Christians within the context of a small group structure. Almost all churches today value the teaching ministry and most of them claim to value teaching within the context of discipleship. However, most research and statistics reveal that the great majority of evangelical Christian churches has little or no formal structure or methodology for forming disciples. As I have previously mentioned, most churches value the ministry of teaching, however the Lord Jesus Christ left specific commands for us as his people to do more than just teach new converts. Teaching new converts produces knowledgeable converts, but in order to make disciples of Christ, we must teach them to obey all the things that he has commanded.

The 12 subjects of this "manual" are basic building blocks for strengthening new Christians and providing them with the opportunity of taking their first steps as disciples of Jesus Christ. However, if this manual is only used as a study guide to teach the new Christian a new set of facts devoid of a discipleship bond, relationship and commitment to grow, the most it can do for new Christians, is help them expand their knowledge level of what a Christian is supposed to do. Jesus never commanded us to teach people what they are supposed to do. He commanded us to make disciples, and to teach them how to do what they are supposed to do. This manual is the "what" that they should do. The "teaching to obey" part is up to the person designated to train the new convert, who teaches the new Christian, using this manual, and the new Christian or "learner", who follows the instructions and does everything within his power to do just as his teacher instructs him.

This is the only method authorized by the Lord Jesus. The word disciple implies being a learner, not a learner like a student is a learner, but a learner like an intern or an apprentice is a learner. Interns and apprentices are not quick-studies. This may come as a shock to you, but in Christ's kingdom there are no quick studies or self-taught leaders, only disciples, interns, and apprentices.

If you are a Christian leader and desire to be used of God to build his kingdom by making and multiplying disciples then this manual is a great place to start under three conditions:

Number one – you are already habitually practicing each one of these 12 disciplines. It's not enough to know and understand what these principles mean. The Pharisees and doctors of the law had sufficient knowledge to know what they were teaching, but they didn't teach with authority because they didn't practice what they taught. When Jesus taught, the people recognized his spiritual authority. He lived what he taught. Unless you have already integrated these disciplines into your character, the best you can be is a Scribe or Pharisee that tells others what they are supposed to do but having no power to teach them the practice of the disciplines.

Number two – you must have followers. If no one is following you then you are not a leader, even if you have the title of leader. The scribes and Pharisees had their titles, but they didn't have many followers.

Number three – you must provide a context within which the new Christians that you are strengthening will be able to practice the disciplines that you are teaching them. In many churches, there are no structures that provide a practical context for the training of disciples. The ideal situation is when the church is organized in small groups that are challenged to grow and multiply by teaching these disciplines to reach more and more generations of new disciples. The life of the small group provides the perfect context for the application of each of these principles.

If you are a new Christian and have a hunger and thirst to grow in God, then this manual is a good place to start, again, under three conditions:

Number one – Someone who is already practicing the 12 disciplines in this manual must agree to train you to practice all 12 disciplines.

Number two – You agree to submit yourself to the directions given by the person who will use this material to teach you how to obey each of the 12 disciplines.

Number three – There is a third element that also must be present. There must be an organic context in which each of these 12 disciplines can be practiced and applied and eventually the disciple becomes the discipler, with the responsibility of repeating the same process which they themselves have gone through in the lives of other new Christians.

CONTENTS

INTRODUCTION

If you are Christian leader, I wish you well in employing these 12 principles in the lives of your disciples! God bless you. If you have any doubts or questions or would like a word of encouragement, visit me at www.thevineusa.com

If you are a new Christian, then congratulations and welcome! You are now part of the family of God!

In Ephesians, the Apostle Paul said:

> *Now, therefore, you are no longer strangers and foreigners, but fellow citizens with the saints and members of the household of God, having been built on the foundation of the apostles and prophets, Jesus Christ himself being the chief corner stone, in whom the whole building, being joined together, grows into a holy temple in the Lord (Ephesians 2:19-21)*

In the natural realm, each person is born with a father, a mother, brothers and sisters, and probably many other relatives. God's plan is that each child be raised in a family. The same is true in God's spiritual family when each new Christian is born again in the spirit. In the same way that our parents, older siblings and relatives played an important role in the early years of our lives, the members of the family of God, the church, will now be a great help in your spiritual growth and development.

During the next few months, we want to offer you the help of a brother or sister who is already part of this family. They are a kind of "Guardian Angel" in human form. These brothers and sisters have the responsibility of looking after you therefore, we encourage you to meet with them each week to share and discuss the lessons of this book.

In addition, we want to stress the need for you to participate in one of our "small groups" which are groups of people from our church family that meet regularly in the homes of some of the members. We often refer to these groups as "Life groups" or "cell groups". Just as the human body is made up of many cells, our church is also composed of many cells which are united together to make up the

"Body of Christ". Through the cells, we can live out and experience the reality of taking part of and participating in the family of God.

When someone first visits one of our worship celebrations, they see many different people worshiping God. They may wonder how someone can be part of a family with so many strangers. The secret is in the dynamics of cell group life. We are a large church that meets in a building on Sundays but also during the week in smaller groups called "cells". Though there are many people that you do not yet know, you do not have to feel overwhelmed, because you will begin by participating in a cell group where you will receive care, love and fellowship and a "guardian angel" to help you along in your new walk with Christ.

We do our best to be a church of the 21st Century that functions in the same pattern as the early Christians did in apostolic times. In those days, they spent much time together as a family and quickly grew together in Christ. The book of Acts shows us that they met for corporate meetings in the temple and in smaller groups in homes.

Acts 2:46,47 says,

> *"So continuing daily with one accord in the temple, and breaking bread from house to house, they ate their food with gladness and simplicity of heart, praising God and having favor with all the people. And the Lord added to the church daily those who were being saved."*

Unfortunately, in many cases, over the centuries the Church has ceased to be a family and has become a mere organization. We have the privilege of entering into the kingdom of God at a time when we as a group of local churches are striving to live as one big family and not just an organization.

Most people use the word "church" to refer to the building where they meet for church services, but the word "church" refers to "the called out" people of God. God has called us out of the world system and its values and has commanded us to serve him, the God who has revealed his values and his will to his people. That is why we have adopted the name "The Vine." In our church we do not say that we are "going to church" when referring to the church building. We say that we are going to the celebration service or the youth meeting, or whatever event that the church has organized. We are the church; the building is simply a place where we meet to practice life in the Vine. The Vine is like a tree, and you are one more branch that God has grafted into his precious vine.

We as Christians all need each other to be a family that grows together for the glory of God. Yes, you are part of this family! If you do not already belong to one of our Life groups, we welcome you to participate in one this week! Enjoy your home! Welcome to the family!

CHAPTER 1

YOU HAVE BEEN BORN AGAIN

In this lesson, you will learn:

• What the new birth is

• How the new birth comes about

• What the signs of a new life with God are

Once you have a personal encounter with God, you realize that something very different has happened to you. Deep down inside you know that you are not the same person that you once were. Of course, on the outside, you still look the same, but inside something revolutionary has happened. The things that appealed to you before, no longer fascinate you. Your friends notice that you are very different and perhaps not even you understand your new outlook on life. God's Word has a name for this experience: the new birth. You have been born again! You are now a new person, a new spiritual creation!

This is the first genuine spiritual experience, the first stage of your Christian life.

What exactly is the meaning of the new birth?

It means that you have received God's divine life, within your already existing natural life. Before, you had only your natural life, but now you have received a spiritual life, the life of God himself. The Bible also calls this experience regeneration.

The salvation of God is extremely full and complete. It includes the forgiveness and cleansing of sins, sanctification, justification, freedom from slavery to sin and regeneration. All of these things have become a reality in your life. However, among all of these spiritual realities, regeneration is the most important because it is the center of our salvation. The central purpose of God in saving us is for us to have his life. It is for that reason that he has forgiven our sins, justified us, sanctified us and set us free. He accomplished all this with a purpose: that you might receive his life within you, through the new birth.

Because we have his life inside of us, we can say that we are the children of God. Every child carries within himself the nature of his father. The same happens to us: we carry the life and nature of God within us, so we are his children. Rejoice! You are now a child of God, with all the rights that this position entails.

The new birth, or regeneration as the Bible calls it, is the entrance of God's life within you. It is the first experience of the Christian life and the starting point of your growth in God. The following points will help you understand more completely how this has happened.

What you were before being born again

The new birth experience relates primarily to four things: our nature, our heart, our spirit and the life of God. We will now examine these four things before you were born again.

First, Jeremiah 17:9 says *"The heart is deceitful above all things, And desperately wicked; Who can know it?"* Although the prophet spoke of the heart, this verse is in fact referring to human nature. Thus, we see that our original human nature is deceptive, fraudulent and extremely corrupt, completely different from the nature of God.

Secondly, your heart was as hard as stone. Ezekiel 36:26 says that man's heart is a heart of stone. This means that before being born again your heart was hard, rebellious and insensitive to the things of God.

Thirdly, your spirit was dead to God, as Ephesians 2:1 declares. Although you always had a spirit, formerly, it was dead to God. It was like a broken radio. It was a radio, but it was unable to tune to any frequency. Your mind was like a broken radio, unable to tune in to God's voice and hear it. Only the human spirit has the ability to make contact with God, but you were dead and so you did not understand the things of the spirit. In fact, they seemed like foolishness to you.

Fourthly, you were separate from God's life. Since the nature of every unregenerate person is corrupt, your heart was hardened toward God and your spirit was dead to him. Therefore you were separated from God's life (Ephesians 4:18). All of this describes the state and condition that you were in before you were born again.

How the new birth occurred

First, at the time you were born again, you woke up to the fact that you had a corrupt nature and had rebelled against God. You had never noticed this tendency before, but at the time of your conversion, the light of God revealed your spiritual condition to you. The Holy Spirit enlighten you and you began to notice that not only what you did was wrong, but that your very nature was wrong.

Secondly, your heart was broken before God. When we are born again, the Holy Spirit enlightens us, and we begin to see our sin against God and man. Because of this light, our heart breaks before God.

Thirdly, your spirit became broken and contrite. Because of the repentance of your heart, God filled your spirit with a godly sorrow because of your sin.

Fourthly, you received God's life within your spirit. God wanted man to experience life way back in the Garden of Eden by eating of the tree of life. However, man sinned and as a result, God cast him out of the Garden placing a Cherub with a flaming sword to guard the way to the tree of life (Genesis 3:24). Because of this, man could no longer have God's life. However, there came a day when Jesus shed his blood on the cross, thereby satisfying the requirement of the justice, glory and holiness of God and thus opened the path that leads to God's life. Thus, when we receive the Lord Jesus Christ with contrition, repentance and faith, we receive God's life in our human spirit (1 John 5:11).

How the new birth has changed you

The four points that we have just outlined are also the unmistakable signs that a person has been born again, and regenerated by the Spirit of God. Now that you have been born again, how are you different from before?

First, you may feel that you still have an earthly and corrupt nature, but you do not want to trust it or allow it to dominate your life.

Secondly, you have received a new heart. This new heart is open and tender toward God. God removed the old heart of stone and now you have a sensitive heart, a heart of flesh as described by the prophet in Ezekiel 36:26. This speaks of a heart that desires to love God and have fellowship with him. A spiritually regenerated heart longs for spiritual things and is willing to obey God's voice. Although it may seem like it is not always able to comply, it has a disposition and a deep yearning to obey.

Thirdly, your spirit became alive to God. Your spirit was formerly dead, but through the new birth, God made it alive by the Holy Spirit. You are now able to communicate with God, hear his voice and understand spiritual things.

Fourthly, you have received God's life. This life must now grow in you and fill your entire being. This life is now the center of your being. To be a Christian means that you have God's life within you. As you grow, you will be more and more sensitive to it and want to obey it even more.

Signs of the new life

In Scripture, we see that the life that God has planned for you is full of joy and rest, with full and constant communion with God in perfect harmony with his will. God offers us a life that has no hunger for the attractions of the world, because it is a life full of God and is an overcoming life that no one or thing can easily shake. In fact, Psalm 125:1 says,

> *"Those who trust in the Lord Are like Mount Zion, Which cannot be moved, but abides forever."*

The new life that you have received is Christ himself; therefore, there is no place for weakness or defeat (Colossians 3:4). Let us look at the practical characteristics of this new life that you have received in your spirit.

It is a life free of sin.

Jesus set you free from sin and now you are now free of the bonds of sin. Matthew quoted the prophet who said,

> *"And she will bring forth a Son, and you shall call his name Jesus, for he will save his people from their sins."* *(Matthew 1:21)*

Being set free from sin does not exclude the possibility that you will eventually stumble, or that you will ever be tempted, but it does mean that you are free to refuse to sin every time the devil tempts you.

It is a life of intimate communion with God

Once you have received a new spirit, this new spirit is full of hunger for the Lord. Therefore, you will have an intense yearning for a deeper intimacy with God.

> *To grant us that we, Being delivered from the hand of our enemies, Might serve him without fear, in holiness and righteousness before him all the days of our life. (Luke 1:74, 75)*

It is a life of satisfaction with the Lord

God's will is that we be satisfied and content. If you still feel an inner lack of satisfaction, you need to evaluate if you have really drunk the true living water, or if you have started drinking the water of the world again. Whoever drinks of the living water that Christ gives has his spiritual thirst quenched, but whoever drinks the water of the world will always thirst for something more in life.

In John 4:14 Jesus said,

> *"Whoever drinks of the water that I shall give him will never thirst. But the water that I shall give him will become in him a fountain of water springing up into everlasting life."*

It is a life full of influence

Because of the new birth, a spiritual river begins to flow from the depths of your being and touches all areas of your life. This river, in addition to satisfying your needs, has the power to influence and touch other people. You now need to let this river flow from inside you to meet other people's needs.

Once Jesus got up and said,

> *"If anyone thirsts, let him come to me and drink. He who believes in me, as the Scripture has said, out of his heart will flow rivers of living water." John 7:37-38.*

It is a life that overcomes the devil and circumstances

All those who have been born again are able to overcome the devil and any adverse circumstance that life may throw in their path. This is because God's life inhabits them now and God's life overcomes all things.

Romans 8:35-37 says,

> *"Who shall separate us from the love of Christ? Shall tribulation, or distress, or persecution, or famine, or nakedness, or peril, or sword? As it is written: "For Your sake we are killed all day long; We are accounted as sheep for the slaughter." Yet in all these things we are more than conquerors through him who loved us".*

It is a life that produces good deeds

Those who are born again have an inner longing to do God's will by fulfilling his Word. They may fail at times, but the longing remains and they eventually end up doing good.

> *For we are his workmanship, created in Christ Jesus for good works, which God prepared beforehand that we should walk in them. (Ephesians 2:10)*

Some practical Tips

• Now that you have been born again, you should be baptized and take the following practical actions:

• Tell your friends and relatives that you are now a regenerated child of God.

• If you have not yet done so, join a cell group where you can fellowship with other Christians.

• Buy a Bible and start reading the New Testament. Ask the person designated as your "guardian angel" for a Bible reading plan to assist you.

• It is vital that you attend every Sunday Church celebration service. This is where you will receive a weekly dose of anointing and God's Word.

• At the end of this book is a series of declarations. Repeat each one of them by choosing one per day. This is not a prayer but a declaration of faith that you repeat to yourself and to the spiritual world. They are part of the written Word of God. Read them aloud and they will fill you with faith.

• You are now a child of God with the right to claim your salvation. You can rest assured of the fact that your salvation is eternally yours.

Nothing can change that fact for all eternity, no matter what happens, you will never cease to be a child of God.

• If you encounter any problem, call the person designated to be your "guardian angel".

CHAPTER 2

ABANDON THE PRACTICES OF THE PAST

In this lesson, you will learn:

- The importance of resolving the sins of your past and abandoning old habits
- Which areas in your life you still need to resolve
- How to deal with things associated with idols, and anything unclean and inappropriate for Christians

Since you have been born again and have become a new creature, you need to resolve certain issues from your past. It is essential that you abandon old ways and cease from the practice of things that are incompatible with God's Word. Without a doubt, you have a number of things from your past that need to be resolved and correctly concluded.

God's Word emphasizes the fact that God has dealt with your past and now you have been sanctified, washed, and justified in the name of the Lord Jesus and in the Spirit of our God (1 Corinthians 6:9-11). Since the Lord has completely dealt with your past, the emphasis of the New Testament always begins with your conversion and focuses on your present and favorable future.

However, in order to move forward you need to conclude your old way of living. The Bible gives use two examples of people who properly concluded their past. The first is Zacchaeus. In Luke 19, after believing on the Lord, he immediately felt the conviction of the Holy Spirit for having financially extorted so many people in his past and for having such a covetous and stingy attitude. Then he told the Lord that whatever he had wrongly taken from others he would restore fourfold. Beyond that, he was willing to give half of his possessions to the poor. That is how he concluded his past and began his new life. The other example is the Ephesian Christians after their conversion from black magic when they brought their books together and burned them in public (Acts 19:19). There is no room for such things in the new life.

It is so important to properly conclude the past and destroy anything that still binds you. After all, you have been born again, and you are a new person.

What needs to be resolved and concluded?

What types of things should you eliminate from your life after being born again? We need to eliminate four categories of things from our past:

- Anything associated with idols
- Evil and impure things
- Unjust things
- Inappropriate things

Anything associated with idols

In God's Word, conversion relates to the forsaking of idols. Paul mentions the example of the Thessalonians that *"turned to God from idols to serve the living and true God." (1 Thessalonians 1:9)*

Remember that now you are the temple of the Holy Spirit, and there can be no communion between God and idols. God's Word clearly warns us in 1 John 5:21 *"Little children, keep yourselves from idols"*

You must realize how God views idolatry in the Scriptures. God forbids making anything in the image of whatever is in the sky, on land or in the sea, and forbids entertaining the slightest thought that such object may be living. If you entertain any such thought, these images can become idols in your life. Of course, the images in themselves do not mean anything, but when a person recognizes them as living entities, they become demonic. The truth is that demons receive the worship of man through such images (Deuteronomy 5:8).

God expressly forbids his children from seeking out such idols even out of curiosity to find out how they are worshiped (Deuteronomy 12:30). What relationship do we who are the temple of God have with idols? The implication is obvious: a child of God should not visit idolatrous temples, except for some very special reason. It is not appropriate to go to such places even for recreational purposes. The command to keep ourselves from idols means to stay away from them.

Avoid mentioning the names of entities and idols unless it is necessary for illustration or teaching (Psalm 16:4). Also, put an end to any kind of superstition and do not entertain the slightest fear of superstitious threats. Many believers still have the idea that some kind of event, object, color, number, palm reading, etc. will govern their fate. The scriptures forbid such things. You must cut off anything related to idolatry in your life permanently and completely.

You should destroy or burn any objects of idol worship used in the past. Do not sell them, donate or give them away, but destroy them. This is very serious because it involves God's zeal for his people. From the moment of conversion, every believer must turn away from idols, and cast out any thought of respect, or reverence to them. God is spirit and he should never be associated with any image.

Finally, it is necessary to break and undo any pact or covenant made in any establishment where voodoo or any other satanic cult is practiced. This should be done prayerfully and in some cases with fasting. Ask your "Guardian Angel" to help you pray about it. God has destroyed all the rights that the devil may have had in your life when you came to Jesus; however, some people have to break these bonds of the past.

The Holy Spirit will show you whether there are objects in your home that you should destroy such as carved or painted images, candles, incense, books, videos, amulets, clothes, ornaments, furniture, etc. The Holy Spirit shows us that the children of God should not have such things in their homes. In Acts 19:19 we see that the Ephesians burned all their books about magic. These books were worth fifty thousand pieces of silver. That is a lot of money, yet none of these books were sold; the former owners who absorbed the loss of potential financial gain in order to resolve their past publicly destroyed them all.

Destroy all impure and evil objects

You should destroy any objects used in idol worship and renounce and reject all evil teaching. Anything that has a clear connection with sin must be destroyed as well as books, CDs and pornographic paraphernalia, or overtly sexual objects that were used in new age ceremonies and evil cults and whatever the Holy Spirit rejects.

There are certain things, like clothes and furniture, for example, that do not necessarily have any intimate connection with sin, but which the Holy Spirit may lead you to destroy and burn, especially if you have used such objects, pieces of furniture or clothing for a long time in the practice of sin.

We can find an example of this in Leviticus 13:14 where we read about how the Israelites were to deal with the clothing of a person who had contracted leprosy. If after an examination, the priest verified that some clothing had been contaminated by leprosy, he was instructed to have them burned. However, other clothes that were not contaminated could be washed and re-used. We can easily apply this instruction when considering what to do with clothes that transvestites or prostitutes have used or clothing used in satanic rituals and Freemasonry. We should burn such clothing because it is intimately associated with and contaminated by sin. Other clothing may still be used with slight alteration or tailoring if it is merely a question of modesty.

You must realize that being a Christian is a very serious matter. It is much more than going to church meetings and listening to good sermons. You must deal with every area of your life recognizing that you should never turn back.

Unjust actions and attitudes must be resolved

Zacchaeus sets a good example in Luke 19:8 of righting wrongs committed against others.

Everything that you have obtained in the past by illegal and unfair means, such as fraud, theft, robbery, finding lost objects without returning them to their rightful owners, failure to return items that you have borrowed, all of these things need to be dealt with in a very specific manner. Even if you do not have the financial means to give back what you have wrongfully taken, you must take responsibility and deal with any unresolved matter of your past. Although none of this will alter God's forgiveness and love revealed through the blood of Jesus on your behalf, responsibly resolving your past will protect you from further discipline from God and will have a definite influence in your testimony before others.

If, for example, you stole a thousand dollars from someone before you were converted, you probably would not be able to preach the gospel to that person without resolving the fraud. You could try to preach the gospel to him, but in his mind, most likely, he would only be able to think of the thousand dollars that you stole. It is true that God would have forgiven you, but you cannot exercise your testimony without resolving the issue. You cannot refuse to pay a debt just because God has forgiven you. This issue is intimately related to your testimony.

Zacchaeus returned the money and it strengthened his testimony and proved his godly fear. At the time, people in the crowd were muttering that Jesus had dined in the home of a sinner. While they complained about how the man had stolen from people, Zacchaeus stood and said,"... whoever I have wronged I will restore to them four times more." His attitude was not a condition for becoming a son of Abraham, nor was it a prerequisite to salvation. Rather, it was the consequence of having become a son of Abraham and the result of salvation having entered his house. Through his attitude, he could sustain his testimony before men and show that he was truly repentant of his sin.

As a new convert, you must ask yourself if you have somehow cheated someone or borrowed something without returning it, or if you have obtained anything through unfair or dishonest means. If this is the case, you should deal with each one of these things. Biblical repentance includes confession and the abandonment of the misconduct.

Inappropriate matters must be resolved

Inappropriate matters are different from improper, unfair or illegal matters. Some things are not appropriate for children of God, even if they are not against the law.

One of the most common examples of this type of situation is the subject of marriage. Many couples live together for years without getting married. Cohabitation is inappropriate for a Christian and must be resolved by either separation, or marriage. Cohabitation must be resolved for the good of the family and the Christian witness since it is clearly contrary to God's Word.

If you have problems with addiction to alcoholic beverages, tobacco and gambling, you must also resolve these issues. These things are legal but inappropriate for a child of God. Such things must be resolved and permanently abandoned.

Another situation that you should deal with is any improper commercial activities. Do not put this off, take care of it promptly, especially if the activity involves the sale of alcoholic beverages or working in a promiscuous atmosphere. As Christians, we should not work in singles clubs as dancers or by sensually exposing our bodies. Do not do anything that compromises your image as a Christian.

Resolve your past and forget about it!

In Philippians 3:13 Paul sets the pattern for us,

> *"Brethren, I do not count myself to have apprehended; but one thing I do, forgetting those things which are behind and reaching forward to those things which are ahead"*

The world's standard and that of psychology, is to remember, but God's standard is to forget. As someone who has been born again you must know and believe that now you have no past. Everything was resolved and forgotten and God has no recollection of your sin. Therefore, forget the mistakes, failures and sins of your past.

Everything that you have properly dealt with through the cross by confession and the willingness to make restitution has been washed by the blood of Jesus and forgotten by God. God has no memory of confessed sins. We should not remind God what he has chosen to forget. The Lord says,

> *"I, even I, am he who blots out your transgressions for My own sake; And I will not remember your sins." (Isaiah 43:25).*

Therefore, once you have concluded and resolved your past, forget it do not let it affect your present life.

Some practical Tips:

- Together with your "guardian angel", go through your house and gather all objects that are associated with idolatry, new age, superstition, magic and pornography. These can be pictures, sculpture, books, CDs, DVDs, or any other object. Take everything to a separate location and burn them. Do not give any of these objects as gifts to anyone, but burn them all.

After burning everything pray together and break the curse with the help of your "guardian angel".

- Look over all of your clothes, CDs and videos and see if there is anything connected to sin whether it is sensuality or the occult. You should burn everything. Break any curse renouncing any link to the past with the help of your "guardian angel".

- If you feel the need, use a checklist for breaking curses caused by sinful practices of the past. Ask your pastor for this and go down the checklist even if you have already participated in an encounter weekend.

- Make a list of objects or assets that you have obtained illegally. Also, make sure that you have returned any borrowed items still in your possession. Return everything that you can think of. Make restitution for everything for which you did not pay. Whatever sin you cannot correct, confess before God together with your "guardian angel".

- See if there are any pending issues in your life like an ungodly relationship or a non-legal separation, illegal activities, inappropriate for a child of God or something of the sort. Resolve all of this before God.

- The sign that you have concluded resolving the past is the peace of God described in Romans 8:5-6. Once the Lord brings peace to your heart, it is because you have successfully dealt with the past. Then forget your past life without God, for it no longer holds any power over your life.

CHAPTER 3

DEALING WITH SIN

In this lesson, you will learn:

- Why we need to deal with known sins
- How to deal with known sins
- How to overcome the practice of sin
- How to overcome temptation

If you truly desire to grow spiritually, you will need to learn how to effectively deal with sin. Once a young man asked a servant of God how to grow in the spiritual life. The servant of God then asked him how many days had gone by since he had dealt with sin.

Learning to deal with sin is therefore a lesson that you must practice for the rest of your life. It is like washing your face or brushing your teeth. You need to learn how to do these things and you must do them every day. If you wash your face for three years and then stop and never wash it again, you will end up with a horrible appearance.

God's Word says much about how to deal with sin.

In Matthew 5:23-26 we read:

> *Therefore if you bring your gift to the altar, and there remember that your brother has something against you, leave your gift there before the altar, and go your way. First be reconciled to your brother, and then come and offer your gift. Agree with your adversary quickly, while you are on the way with him, lest your adversary deliver you to the judge, the judge hand you over to the officer, and you be thrown into prison. Assuredly, I say to you, you will by no means get out of there till you have paid the last penny.*

In this passage the expressions to "be reconciled to" and "agree with" mean to deal with the sin that we have committed against our brother.

In 1 John 1:9 we read:

> *If we confess our sins, he is faithful and just to forgive us our sins and to cleanse us from all unrighteousness.*

In Proverbs 28:13 we read:

> *He who covers his sins will not prosper, But whoever confesses and forsakes them will have mercy.*

From these verses, we can perceive that God requires us to deal with our sin in three ways:

- By reconciling ourselves with the person against whom we have sinned
- By confessing it before God
- By abandoning it

The goal in dealing with sin

When the word "sin" appears in the singular form in the Bible it refers to the sin nature inside of us, or what we may call "the principle of sin". This principle will be with us as long as we live in the body. Only at the resurrection, will we finally be freed from it. However, when the word "sins" appears in the plural form it refers to sinful acts that we commit. In relation to our "sins", we are responsible to resolve them before God and before others.

Each sin that we commit of which we do not repent or confess will be written down before God. In the future, God will judge us according to what has been recorded. Whether we perceive it or not, our sins generally affect other people. Therefore, besides the fact that they will be recorded before God, they also create problems with other people.

Therefore, dealing with sin should involve these two aspects: The record of sin before God and the problems caused for other people. On one hand, we need the forgiveness of God, and on the other hand, we need reconciliation with the people against whom we have sinned. When we do this, we are responsibly dealing with sin.

The basis for dealing with sin

In order to maintain communion with God we must deal with the sins that the Holy Spirit reveals to our conscience. For example, we may have committed many sins, but when we enter into communion with God, we only remember some of them. We must therefore deal with these. If we remember ten sins then we must properly deal with the ten sins. We must deal with only the sins that we remember. We have already learned in Matthew that if you remember sinning against someone, you must deal with it immediately. However, if you do not remember anything your fellowship with God will not be broken.

We do not need to deal with sins of which our conscience does not accuse us. This does not mean that we have no sin, But that God only deals with us based on our conscience. As we advance in our fellowship with God, his light will reveal the sins that we do not see.

Sometimes other people will be conscious of a sin that you yourself do not perceive. As a result, your conscience does not accuse you and your fellowship with God can continue without being affected. However, whenever you are conscious of a sin and do not deal with it, your conscience will accuse you and you cannot maintain fellowship with God. According to Matthew 5, if you remember a sin that you have committed and do not deal with it, it will immediately interrupt your fellowship with God.

The more fellowship you have with God, the more sensitive you will be to sin. Some people, when they go to pray, do not even remember the mistakes that they committed because their fellowship with God is superficial and therefore the light that they receive is weak. When you are in a dark room, you think that the air is clean, but once the light of the sun enters into the room you perceive how much dust is floating in the air.

In the same way, dealing with sin depends on a sensitive conscience, and your fellowship with the Lord depends on the extent of the sensitivity of your conscience. If you have deep fellowship with God, your conscience will be sensitive and strong. On the other hand, if your fellowship is superficial, your conscience will be clouded and confused.

Therefore, never evaluate other people based on the criteria of your own personal conscience; nor accept the conscience of others as criteria to judge yourself. Learn to deal with sin only in accordance with your own conscience within the context of your fellowship with the Lord.

However, be careful! If your conscience does not accuse you for something clearly condemned by God's Word, it is a sign that you have not yet been born again.

How to deal with sin

Dealing with the record of sin

God makes the remission of your sin based on the redemptive work of his Son the Lord Jesus Christ on the cross. Every record of sin is erased before God by the blood of Christ. Our Lord suffered the righteous and divine judgment that was meant for you. His blood satisfied the demands of God's law on your behalf.

However, for this fact to become a personal reality, it is necessary for you to appropriate or to apply it. This application happens in two parts: for the sins that you have committed before converting and for the sins that you committed after conversion. The sins that were committed before you were saved, have been forgiven by faith. This is what we read in Acts 10:43,

> *"To him all the prophets witness that, through his name, whoever believes in him will receive remission of sins."*

To erase the record of sins that you have committed you need only believe. If you have believed on the Lord, they have already been erased.

However, after your conversion it is a little different. It is not enough to believe, it is necessary also to confess.

> *If we confess our sins, he is faithful and just to forgive us our sins and to cleanse us from all unrighteousness. (1 John 1:9)*

These words were written to believers therefore in order for your sins to be forgiven after conversion, you must confess them before God. Forgiveness now depends on your confession.

If you do not confess your sins, God will not purify you nor forgive them, but at the moment you do so, you will receive forgiveness and purification. If you confess while you are still here on the Earth, you will receive forgiveness here on the Earth. Otherwise, you will have to do it in the coming kingdom before the judgment seat of Christ. Therefore, do not allow un-confessed sin to remain in your life.

Dealing with sinful acts

How should you deal with sinful acts? If you have offended God, confess it and ask his forgiveness. If besides sinning against God, you sinned against a person, you should resolve this with the person, asking for his forgiveness.

If your sin against a person involves merely a moral matter, you need only confess it and ask the person for forgiveness, but if money or material damages are involved, you should then pay the amount that you owe or the value of the damages.

This is the general principle, but I would like to give you four rules to follow in order to deal with sin:

First, you should go to the offended person and resolve the matter. If you have only sinned against God, resolve it with him alone. If you have sinned against God and the person, resolve it with both of them.

It is unnecessary to involve anyone against whom you have not sinned and is not part of the solution. If you confess your sin to other people or to those who have no knowledge of your sin, you will not only leave them with a bad impression, but you will also give them an opportunity to gossip and may cause more damage to the person offended.

Second, you should deal with the sin according to the circumstances in which you have sinned. If you have sinned publicly, resolve it publicly; if not, take care of it privately. The sin committed in private does not need to be dealt with openly unless it becomes known and causes a scandal. If you have sinned against a person who is not aware of it, you do not need to deal with it face-to-face. It is sufficient to deal with it on your own.

If for example, you stole from someone, but the person did not notice it, you do not have to announce it publicly; it is enough to resolve it secretly and return what you have stolen. If you have hated someone secretly, you do not need to confess it to the person, it is enough to repent of it internally. If you confess your hateful feelings to the person, you may produce an unnecessary problem and make things worse. However, if you hate someone and this becomes common knowledge, then you must seek the person and confess your sin, in such a way that the barrier is eliminated.

Third, when you deal with sin, only deal with those for which you are personally responsible. Do not ever involve other people. For example, you and another person committed a sin together. When you go to resolve the sin, do not denounce or expose the other person, merely resolve your part and allow the other person to resolve his part.

Fourth, if the sin you have committed involves valuable objects or material damages to another person, you should make restitution. It is necessary to make restitution for that which you have taken or for damages that you have caused. If there is no way that you can pay damages, at least seek out the person who suffered damages, confess your sin and ask for forgiveness. If you are able to make restitution then do so.

The goal of restitution should naturally be the well-being of the person that has suffered damages. However, if the person has already died or lives in an unknown location, pay the debt or damages to a close relative. If you cannot localize a relative, you should give an offering to God (Numbers 5:7, 8). The representative of God on the earth is the church; therefore, restitution given to God should be brought to the local church.

In conclusion, the purpose of dealing with sin is so that you maintain a clear conscience and freedom from guilt. Whenever God gives you light, make yourself available to deal with the sin, whatever it may be, not caring about your image before men nor considering the price to be paid.

How to overcome sin

Sin does not just happen by chance; it is the fruit of a process. In this process, Satan will try to awaken your carnal nature so that you do something against God's life in your spirit. If you understand this part of the process, then you can overcome it. The process of sin involves five stages: first, the enemy gets your attention, next he awakens a natural instinct within you, then this instinct becomes a desire, the desire becomes an intention and finally, an intention becomes a sinful act.

Attention

In the first stage, the devil will try to get your attention through your physical senses; sight, sound and touch. He shows you something that he believes you will find interesting and will want to do. If you really want the victory over this temptation, it is necessary to stop the process at this point. Therefore, it is important that you avoid places, people and circumstances that may cause you to sin. Jesus taught that:

> *If your right eye causes you to sin, that you should pluck it out and cast it from you. (Matthew 5:29)*

What Jesus meant to say is that if a friendship makes you sin, whether it be a girlfriend or boyfriend get rid of it. If television makes you sin, get rid of it. In the fight against sin, it is necessary to be radical with anything that causes you to sin.

Instinct

After the enemy gets your attention, he will then attempt to awaken your natural instincts. What are these instincts? Instincts are innate natural tendencies that God himself created within us. We do not need to learn how to activate our instincts; they have always been latent within us since we were born. For example, we possess instincts of survival, for this reason; there is no need for us to learn how to nurse as babies. We are born knowing how to nurse. We were also born with sexual and defensive instincts. The enemy tempts us based on such instincts.

After the enemy gets your attention, he will awaken one or more of your instincts. Suppose that God said, "Thou shall not eat pizza!" Of course, he never gave such a command but just imagine he did for sake of example. Therefore, the devil comes and he puts a delicious looking pizza in front of you. He gets your attention by the sight and smell. At this point, you should flee, but instead, you become paralyzed, and then, involuntarily your mouth starts to water. This is your instinct. It is not yet sin and you can still flee. However, some people think that you have already sinned just because your mouth started watering; therefore, they give up and stop fighting. Don't do that! Temptation is not sin! All of us will be tempted, but we must resist all temptation.

Desire

The instinct, once awakened, becomes desire. If you have not dealt with the problem at this stage then it will become more difficult. Desire is a temptation that has advanced to the next level. At this point, you will only overcome with the help of another person so it is necessary to seek immediate help from the person designated as your guardian angel. But you can still overcome this temptation because God's Word affirms:

> *God is faithful and will not permit you to be tempted beyond your strength; but together with the temptation, will give you a way of escape so that you may be able to bear it 1 Corinthians 10:13.*

Intention and action

At this stage, the sin has already been committed in the heart. This is when desire has become intention. Desire is different from intention. We may have a desire and in a heated conflict, struggle against it. However, when the desire becomes intention, it is because we have already decided to sin. In God's eyes, intention is equal to action. Jesus said, in Matthew 5:28 that any man who looks at a woman with an impure intention in his heart he has already committed adultery with her in his heart. The only solution now is to confess the sin and abandon it, as I previously stated.

Flight and isolation

After Adam sinned, he hid among the trees of the garden. The same thing often happens today, with each one of us. The first reaction after sinning is to hide. It may be that you stop going to church services and, when you do go, you isolate yourself. You avoid the other members of your cell group and you attempt to hide from God. This is a tactic of the devil used to keep you in sin. Break these chains! If you have sinned, confess the sin immediately and seek out fellowship with God and with the church for your own protection.

Some practical advice

There are no formulas for overcoming sin. As you grow in your knowledge of God, and permit the Holy Spirit to lead you, little by little you will be able to control the process described above. However, you must adopt certain attitudes in order to overcome temptation and sin:

* Recognize the terrible consequences of sin.

"For the wages of sin is death, but the gift of God is eternal life in Jesus Christ our Lord." (Romans 6:23)

• Remember that whatever you plant you will also reap. If you plant sin, you will reap death.

Do not be deceived, God is not mocked; for whatever a man sows, that he will also reap. (Galatians 6:7)

• Yield your entire being to God. In addition, recognize that the members of your body do not belong to you anymore.

For just as you presented your members as slaves of uncleanness, and of lawlessness leading to more lawlessness, so now present your members as slaves of righteousness for holiness. (Romans 6:19)

• Flee from sin. Avoid any thing, situation or person that awakens the desires of your flesh and seek to strengthen your spirit with prayer, bible reading and fellowship with the members of your church family.

And do not present your members as instruments of unrighteousness to sin, but present yourselves to God as being alive from the dead, and your members as instruments of righteousness to God. (Romans 6:13)

• Say no to sin. You can do this because you are no longer a slave of sin.

But now having been set free from sin, and having become slaves of God, you have your fruit to holiness, and the end, everlasting life. (Romans 6:22)

• Pray for victory. Whenever you are tempted, cry out! That is right, cry out loudly for the Holy Spirit to help you.

Watch and pray, lest you enter into temptation. The spirit indeed is willing, but the flesh is weak (Matthew 26:41)

• Resist the devil. You can overcome him, resist and he will flee from you. Never give up. The enemy wants to make you feel defeated, but he is the defeated one. You are an overcomer in Christ Jesus.

Therefore submit to God. Resist the devil and he will flee from you. (James 4:7)

- Renew your mind through the reading of the Bible. Reject wrong thinking when these thoughts come into your head. You can control them. You cannot prevent a bird from landing on your head, but you can stop it from making a nest.

And do not be conformed to this world, but be transformed by the renewing of your mind, that you may prove what is that good and acceptable and perfect will of God. (Romans 12:2)

- When you confess your sin to a counselor or a more mature brother or sister, the chances of repeating the same sin are greatly reduced. James 5:16 says,

Confess your trespasses to one another, and pray for one another, that you may be healed. The effective, fervent prayer of a righteous man avails much.

- Consider yourself dead to sin. The Bible says that you have died to sin and to the world so, believe it! Moreover, act on it. God said it and it is so!

For sin shall not have dominion over you, for you are not under law but under grace. (Romans 6:14)

CHAPTER 4

CONSECRATE YOURSELF TO GOD

In this lesson, you will learn:

- The motive for consecration
- The meaning of consecration
- The importance of consecration
- The basis of consecration
- A practical way to consecration

After getting to know your new position as a child of God, resolving your past and learning to deal with sin, you need to consecrate yourself to God so that you can be edified and grow spiritually. You should not wait too long to do this, because growth begins with consecration.

Many people fail to consecrate themselves to God because they make the mistake of thinking that their conversion is the only thing there is to Christianity. Even a king, once he is converted, needs to place his crown before the feet of the Lord. You must understand from now on, that you are the one that benefited from the Lord when you became his servant and his child.

Consecration involves four principal points: the basis, the motivation, the significance, and the goal.

The basis of consecration is the purchase price

There must be a basis for everything we do. For example, when we move into a house, the basis for doing so is the purchase or the rental agreement. The rental or purchase agreement of a home is the legal foundation that permits us to live there. When a creditor brings a case against someone to obtain the payment of a debt, he can do so because the law supports his case. The debt is the basis for claiming the payment.

God is the god of legality and justice. He never does anything or makes a claim to anything without a just cause. Therefore, when God requires you to consecrate yourself to him, it cannot be without foundation. He has a very solid basis for this: the purchase of your life. The biblical word for the purchase that God made with the price of Christ's blood is called redemption. He bought you; therefore, he can require your consecration.

> *For you were bought at a price; therefore glorify God in your body and in your spirit, which are God's. (1 Corinthians 6:20)*

Your consecration is based on the fact that you belong to God. If we go to a bookstore and we want a book, we cannot just go and pick it up; we have no basis for this since it does not belong to us. However, if we pay the price, we can demand that the book be handed over to us, because it is now our property. The basis of consecration works in exactly the same way. On what basis can God demand you to consecrate yourself to him? The answer is that he purchased you.

The price that he paid for you was very high. The Father purchased you with the blood of Jesus Christ shed on the cross (1 Peter 1:19 and 1 Corinthians 6:20). For this reason, you can say that you are very important to God. If the value of something is determined by the price paid for it, then, we can say that we have enormous value, because we were bought with the most expensive and precious thing: the blood of Jesus.

You are God's property, so whether you feel like it or not, you must consecrate yourself to him. To consecrate yourself is to recognize that you now have an owner; you cannot use your body as you wish, because now it belongs to God. You cannot do whatever you want with your life, because now it belongs to God. He is your owner and your Lord.

In each situation or choice that you need to make, you should pray saying,

> *Lord, I am your purchased slave. You have property rights over me. I belong to you, therefore, I dare not decide anything for myself, but ask you to decide for me.*

This is the correct basis for consecration.

The motive for consecration is God's love

The basis for consecration is a legal matter, the purchase, but the motivation is love. To be saved, you must believe, but in order to grow in God, you need to be won over by him, and love him.

I remember hearing a story of a time when boys used to make their own toys that speaks of a poor boy that made a little car out of tin cans. That toy brought him much happiness. The boy went from place to place with the car and was very proud of what he had done. The car was his masterpiece and it belonged to him. However, one day, someone stole his toy car. How sad! It was un-substitutable.

However walking through the neighborhood days later, the boy saw his little car. It was almost unrecognizable. An ill-mannered neighbor boy, the one who had stolen it had not taken care of the little car, leaving it disfigured and broken. He tried to get his toy car back, but the other boy did not want to give it back. So he bought his little toy car back from the boy who stole it. After purchasing it, he fixed it up, and made it better than it was before. In addition, every time he picked the car up he would say, "Now you belong to me two times, first because I made you and second because I bought you."

Can you see that this is your story? You are doubly the Lords, first because he created you, and second because he bought you back from the hands of the devil, who had robbed you. This simple act shows that God's love for us has no limits.

God does not want you to consecrate yourself to him out of obligation, but out of love. He wants to win over your heart so that you yourself want to be a prisoner of his love.

In 2 Corinthians 5:14, 15, we read:

> *For the love of Christ compels us, because we judge thus: that if One died for all, then all died; and he died for all, that those who live should live no longer for themselves, but for him who died for them and rose again.*

In other words, God's love exerts a strong attraction that compels you to consecrate yourself to him.

As was stated before, consecration is based on a purchase, but it is motivated by love. It is like in marriage. The husband does not feel content when his wife yields herself only out of obligation, but is thrilled when she does this out of love. Jesus is our groom and as such, has rights over us. However, we yield ourselves to him out of love.

The meaning of consecration: present yourself as living sacrifice

Romans 12:1 gives us the precise definition of consecration when it says:

> *I beseech you therefore, brethren, by the mercies of God, that you present your bodies a living sacrifice, holy, acceptable to God, which is your reasonable service.*

This verse shows us that the meaning of consecration is to offer ourselves as a living sacrifice. But, what does that mean? Let us examine three aspects of doing this.

In the first place, the sacrifice involved everything that was placed upon the altar for the exclusive use of God. Those who consecrate themselves must turn over total control of their lives to the hand of God.

In the second place, sacrifices were offerings or presents that were brought to God. When you consecrate yourself, you give yourself as a present to God. In this way, we become God's property first because he created us, next because he bought us and, finally, because we gave ourselves to him as gifts. Such a sacrifice in the form of a present is for the satisfaction of God. Do you want to please God's heart? Then give him a present: consecrate yourself.

Finally, sacrifice also speaks of surrender. God never takes anything by force, since everything must be offered to him voluntarily. We are the ones who spontaneously place ourselves on the altar without daring to get off. Other people can do whatever they want, according to their own will, but we do not live according to the desires of our flesh. Other people can flee from the will of God, but we choose to be prisoners of his love.

The goal of consecration is to serve God

Seeing that the meaning of consecration is to become a sacrifice, a gift to God, then whatever we offer is completely dedicated to him. The goal of consecration is therefore to make ourselves available to

God in order to serve him.

However, to work for God, it is necessary that you allow him to first work in you. Only those who allow themselves to be molded by God can serve him. Through consecration, you allow God to work in you so that, in the end, you can work for him.

Once a gift has been given to God, he will use it in whatever way he pleases. No one can be useful to God without first consecrating him or herself to him, since the Lord only uses that which has been delivered into his hands.

You must present your whole body to God. Just say:

> *From now on, my ears are no longer available to hear anyone else's voice, my hands are no longer available to do anyone else's will, and my feet are no longer available to walk in anyone else's paths. No one but the Lord may use me. I am entirely dedicated to the service of God.*

There is an interesting detail in the meaning of the word consecration. In the original, it means, "to have your hands full". The believer who has his hands full of God cannot be used for any other thing.

Practical advice

- Specifically consecrate each part of your body for the exclusive use of God. Declare that the members of your body are his: your ears are for hearing him, your mouth is for speaking his word, your hands to for serving him and so forth. Ask the person designated as your guardian angel to anoint your hands and your feet as a sign of your consecration to God.

- Ask your Guardian Angel to teach you a song about consecration to the Lord. Sing it during the week.

- Make a list of your projects, dreams, ambitions, possessions and surrender everything into God's hands, mentioning them one by one. Ask the Holy Spirit to confirm the need to do this by filling you with peace.

- Seek out the leader of your cell group and make yourself available to serve the church in whatever way necessary. Remember that the church is the body of Christ. We serve God by serving his body.

- If you have small children, bring them to the celebration service on the day of the Lord's Supper for them to be consecrated and presented to the Lord. Remember to consecrate your family.

Public declaration

I _____ voluntarily declare that I have been purchased by the blood of the Lord Jesus.

From this day forward, I recognize Jesus as my legitimate owner and Lord. Everything that I have and am I have surrendered to him, making him my legal owner to do with me as he pleases.

CHAPTER 5

LEARN TO FORGIVE

In this lesson, you will learn:

- The meaning of forgiveness and how to identify true forgiveness
- The negative consequences of resentment
- What to do when you offend someone and when someone offends you

Forgiveness is extremely important because it demonstrates a very serious spiritual principle: God will forgive you according to the way that you forgive others.

Jesus said:

> *For if you forgive men their trespasses, your heavenly father will also forgive you. But if you do not forgive men their trespasses, neither will your father forgive your trespasses. (Matthew 6:14, 15)*

Therefore, God forgives us if we forgive those who have offended us. Besides this, he wants us to treat each other the way that he has treated us, as we read in Ephesians:

> *. . . And be kind to one another, tenderhearted, forgiving one another, even as God in Christ forgives you. (Ephesians 4:32)*

The only barrier mentioned by the Lord that can keep God from hearing your prayers is your bitterness and resentment towards other people, and especially towards fellow Christians.

If you do not forgive others, neither will God forgive you. Why is that? Is it not true that God bases his forgiveness on his grace? The problem is that when you refuse to forgive others you are implicitly placing yourself in a position of blamelessness and perfection thus feeling qualified to demand perfection from others. Consequently, thinking that you are perfect, you imagine that you have left the position of a sinner and no longer need the grace of God. In this way, there is no forgiveness for you because God only forgives sinners.

A demonic spirit provokes a profound sense of self-righteousness in people that breeds the desire for revenge. We can observe how this spirit operates when we see certain action films. The "bad guy" commits such exaggerated atrocities that we feel a sense of self-righteousness and begin to develop the desire to seek vengeance exacted against him. Then when the "good guy" acts just like the "bad guy", we justify it because of the spirit of vengeance, and we want to see the "good guy" avenge the evil of the "bad guy".

You cannot demand justice because you yourself are not holy. Since all of us are sinners, we do not have the right to demand justice from anyone. That is why we must simply forgive and forget the mistakes that others have committed against us.

When I decide not to forgive, I remove myself from the possibility of forgiveness, because the forgiveness of God is only for those who admit that they are sinners. Upon making such a decision, I am declaring myself righteous and therefore, I miss the forgiveness that comes from God. That is why the Lord said that if we do not forgive others, neither will he forgive us.

> *For if you forgive men their trespasses, your heavenly father will also forgive you. But if you do not forgive men their trespasses, neither will your father forgive your trespasses. (Matthew 6:14, 15)*

What you should do when someone sins against you

Since God has freely forgiven you, you also must freely forgive others.

- You should never hold resentment against anyone, even if you feel that it is justifiable.
- Do not wait for the repentance of the other person, before you forgive them.
- Do not nurse resentment in your heart, deal with it right away.

Resentment produces slavery

The lack of forgiveness keeps you in slavery for the following reasons:

- Resentment is one of the causes of sickness.
- Resentment produces spiritually evil strongholds. For example, bitterness is more than resentment it is a spiritual fortress. Bitterness is an unresolved resentment from the past.
- Resentment turns you into a slave of the person that has offended you. Your thinking and your actions are always a function of your resentment.

What to do if you have offended someone

Therefore if you bring your gift to the altar, and there remember that your brother has something against you, leave your gift there before the altar, and go your way. First be reconciled to your brother, and then come and offer your gift. Agree with your adversary quickly, while you are on the way with him, lest your adversary deliver you to the judge, the judge hand you over to the officer, and you be thrown into prison. Assuredly, I say to you, you will by no means get out of there till you have paid the last penny. (Matthew 5:23-26)

Being cast into prison here can mean several things. It could mean that, if you offend a brother and do not resolve the problem before he dies, God will have to deal with the situation on Judgment Day. This can also imply the manifestation of physical sickness and mental illness that can be a heavy burden in your life.

The lack of forgiveness provides a legal basis for the establishment of evil strongholds in your life.

What should the offended person do?

The first thing is to go to your brother. Jesus said that if your brother sins against you, go to him and tell him his fault between you and him alone (Matthew 18:15).

Do not mention your hurts or resentments to other people, take them to the Lord and deal with them as he has instructed, if you need help or counsel on how to do this then talk to your small group leader.

Jesus said that if your brother sins against you and repents, you should forgive him as many times as necessary.

If your brother sins against you, rebuke him; and if he repents, forgive him. And if he sins against you seven times in a day, and seven times in a day returns to you, saying, 'I repent,' you shall forgive him. (Luke 17:3, 4)

Do not wait for the person that has sinned against you to repent before forgiving him. Jesus and Steven forgave before any attitude of repentance on their offender's part. Both the perpetrators who sin and the victims of sin should seek reconciliation.

Forgiveness does not guarantee restoration of relationship

Jesus said:

If your brother sins against you, rebuke him; and if he repents, forgive him. (Luke 17:3)

Therefore, we must forgive those who sin against us in any situation, but the restoration of those who sin against us to the former level of relationship can only happen when they repent. Suppose that someone asks you for a loan of $1000. After a long time the debtor still does not pay you, and does not even give you an excuse for failing to pay. Should you forgive him? Of course you should. However, if he comes again to ask for more money should you loan it to him? In this case, you forgive him, but you do not need to loan him more money, because he has never repented of the sin that he committed against you by not paying the debt that he agreed to.

Practical advice

- Abandon every worldly attitude. Generally, in the world, we judge others by their actions, but we judge ourselves by our intentions. We want everyone to know that it was not our intention to do anything wrong, but we ignore the excuses of others. Learn to be more accepting of the excuses of others.

- It is common for us to demand justice of others, but for ourselves we want mercy. Maybe it would be better to invert this order. Be hard on yourself and tolerant with the faults of other people.

- Forgiveness is a decision and not a feeling. Decide to forgive and feelings of mercy will come afterward. Do not wait to have holy amnesia. You will still remember the offense of the other person, but deal with it permanently through forgiveness.

- Abandon every feeling of self-righteousness. Recognize that you are a sinner. As such, you do not have any right to demand perfection from anyone.

- Rebuke the spirit of revenge that tries to establish a stronghold over your life. Ask for the person designated as your guardian angel to help you in prayer and in rebuking every evil spirit.

- Ask God to show you how he sees the aggressor. If you see him as God sees him, you will begin to feel as God feels.

- Decide that you will never again mention the offense to another person. To forgive is to forget and we only forget when we stop talking about the subject.

- Release the blessing of God over the person that has offended you.

CHAPTER 6

LEARN HOW TO PRAY

In this lesson, you will learn:

- How to use the prayer that Jesus taught his disciples
- The elements of an effective prayer
- Practical advice on how to pray

The promises concerning prayer are among the most sensational of the entire Bible. Jesus said:

> *If you abide in Me, and My words abide in you, you will ask what you desire, and it shall be done for you. (John 15:7)*

Can you imagine being able to ask God for whatever you want? It is as if you had a blank check signed by God himself. You can then see that learning how to pray is one of the most important things in the Christian life.

Jesus once taught his disciples how to pray. We refer to the prayer that he modeled for them as "the Lord's Prayer". Many people repeat this prayer every day in a religious and mechanical manner, without even knowing what they are saying. However, this was not what the Lord had in mind when he taught it. This prayer is a model for how we should spend our time with God. We should follow this pattern whenever we pray. Use it in your daily prayers, paying attention to the following elements of prayer:

Communion – Our Father in heaven

A Jew could never refer to God as father, but by faith, you are in Christ, and have been made a child of God and can enter into his presence with boldness, calling him Father. To the world, he is the Lord God but to you, he is Father.

Paul says that we should even call him daddy, revealing a deep intimacy with him:

> *For you did not receive the spirit of bondage again to fear,*
> *but you received the Spirit of adoption by whom we cry out,*
> *"Abba, father". (Romans 8:15)*

"Abba, Father" means daddy.

Praise and worship – Hallowed be your name

To make holy means to separate, to place the name of God above all and any other. However, what is God's name?

In the Old Testament, God revealed himself to Moses as "I am". As if he were saying, "I am everything that you need." This expression in Hebrew is Jehovah. The correct pronunciation is unknown: some people say Yahweh others Jehovah.

The Old Testament teaches us that God's people can come to him on the basis of several redemptive names. When you pray, sanctify one of these names each day, according to your need. For example, if you are sick, sanctify the name Jehovah Rapha, which means the Lord is our healer.

Names are important in the Bible, because they express the character of the person, and we know that God cannot deny his name. Therefore, we direct our prayers of faith to him. God will bless us if we sanctify his name and honor him exalting and confessing his name in a loud voice. Do not use the Lord's name in vain, and do not tolerate jokes involving his name.

When the Lord says, "I am", it is covering all of these meanings and much more.

A crying out – your kingdom come

We must ask for the coming of the kingdom or the government of God. He needs to manifest himself in your personal life, in your family, in your church and in your nation.

We know that after Satan's fall, the earth fell under his usurping hand. God created man to take it back, but he sinned, the evil one legitimately gained control of it as a result.

Then, Jesus came to establish his kingdom on the earth. Today this kingdom is restricted to us, his church, but the time will come when his rule will spread over all the earth.

Intercession – your will be done

To be a disciple it is necessary to obey the will of the master. To be part of the kingdom it is necessary to submit to the will of the sovereign King. Many Christians still rule over their own lives and act according to their own thoughts.

You must pray every day in order to know God's will in all areas of your life. Ask God to help you do this.

Petition – give us this day our daily bread

Here the bread represents both our material and our spiritual supply. We know that the Lord does not want us to worry about tomorrow, therefore he directs us to ask for bread each day.

Understand that God is concerned about your supply. There is nothing too big that he cannot do, nor any detail too small yet important to us that is not also important to him.

DECLARE WHO GOD IS!	
The eight redemptive names of God	
Jehovah-Shammah	"The God who is here" – Ezekiel 48:35 *You are always with me! I am not alone!*
Jehovah-Raah	The Lord is my Shepherd – Psalm 23:1 *I shall not want!*
Jehovah-Jireh	"God is my provider" – Genesis 22:14 *You meet all of my needs*
Jehovah-Rapha	"God is my healer" - Exodus 15:26 *Who heals all of my diseases!*
Jehovah-Tsid-kenu	"God is my justice" – Jeremiah 23:6 *In you, I am righteous!*
Jehovah-Mekaddesh	"God is my sanctification" – Leviticus 20:8 *You make me Holy just like Jesus!*
Jehovah-Shalom	"God is my peace" – Leviticus 20:8 *You give me peace in the middle of conflict!*
Jehovah-Nissi	God is my banner - Leviticus 20:8 *You are my victory!*

Bitterness and resentment in your heart are the only barriers that can come between you and the Lord and the answers to your prayers.

If you do not forgive others, neither will God forgive you.

This is a very important point, because if you refuse to forgive, God will not hear your prayers and you will not be able to remain in fellowship with him. He will refuse to hear you until you resolve the matter. Therefore, practice forgiveness as a lifestyle. Forgive daily.

We are all sinners and none of us has the right to demand perfection from anyone. Therefore, our forgiveness is simply forgetting the error of another, just as God has done with us.

Protection – and do not lead us into temptation

Jesus was tempted and tested, and you will be tested in the same way. The tests will come so be prepared for them. The way to prepare yourself is to ask God to spare you from temptation and from a fall.

Be aware that you will be tempted with evil and sinful desires. Humble yourself and recognize that you cannot overcome them in your own strength. If you ask the Holy Spirit to help you he will give you the victory. The best way to ask for help is in a loud voice. Try crying out to the Lord and you will see the manifestation of his power.

Spiritual warfare – but deliver us from the evil one

You must understand that you are in the middle of a spiritual war. God's army (the church) is on one side, the devil, the seducer and tempter is on the other side. For this reason, you must pray so that you do not fall when you are tempted. However, you must recognize that the enemy is a destroyer and in every way possible, he will try to destroy your comfort, your joy, your life, your family and everything else. Therefore, pray every day for God's protection.

Surrender – yours is the kingdom, power and glory

The kingdom, the power and the glory are the main things for which man seeks. They reflect our ego's desire, and that is why we seek them. Our ego wants to be God and in order to resist it; we must deliver everything into God's hands.

What is the kingdom? The kingdom speaks of possessions, riches, respect and recognition. Every person seeks these things and can even become offended when they do not obtain them. Each one of us wants to build our own little personal kingdom, thinking in this way that we will find fulfillment. Therefore, we must surrender our own personal kingdom to God.

What is power? It is an intimate desire to be recognized and to tell others what to do. Many times, we would like to be able to say, "Go to so-and-so and tell them that I was the one who said such and such." Being able to order others around fulfills our ego and shows others that we are important and well known. Power also involves gifts and abilities, leading us to think that we can do things that other people cannot do, or that we are more capable than they are. Such thoughts make us feel happy and fulfilled. Therefore, we must surrender all of our abilities and positions to God.

Finally, we seek after glory, which, just as receiving compliments and having fame, is very important to our ego. However, we know that glory belongs only to God. In Philippians 2:5-8, we read that the Lord himself surrendered his glory, emptying himself of his divine attributes and lived among us. In the same way, those who follow him must take up their cross, or in other words surrender the kingdom, the power, and personal glory.

The reason that we must confess that the power, the glory and the honor belong to God is because all of us unconsciously seek after these things. For this reason, we must confess, every day, that all of these things belong to God.

The Lord teaches us this level of praise and genuine worship through his example of prayer when we allow him to deal deeply with our ego and human independence.

Practical advice

- Pray in the name of Jesus.

  Until now you have asked nothing in my name. Ask, and you will receive, that your joy may be full. (John 16:24)

- Do not permit the presence of any known or un-confessed sin when you pray.

  If I regard iniquity in my heart, the Lord will not hear." (Psalm 66:18)

- Always pray in faith.

  And whatever things you ask in prayer, believing, you will receive. (Matthew 21:22)

- Pray according to God's Word.

   Now this is the confidence that we have in him, that if we ask anything according to his will, he hears us. And if we know that he hears us, whatever we ask, we know that we have the petitions that we have asked of him. (1 John 5:14-15)

- You are before the King. Ask him for big things, because his grace and his power are such that nothing that we could ask of him could be too much.

- You can pray by yourself but prayer in agreement with another person is very powerful.

   And again I say to you that if two of you agree on earth concerning anything that they ask, it will be done for them by my father in heaven. (Matthew 18:19)

- Pray constantly

   Pray without ceasing. (1 Thessalonians 5:17)

- Do not use written prayers, pray spontaneously. Written prayers are repetitious and tend to distance us from God. Spontaneous prayer comes directly from the heart.

   And when you pray do not use vain repetitions as the heathen do. For they think that they will be heard for their many words. (Matthew 6:7)

- Pray the Word. Use the Bible as if it was a book of prayers to God. However, remember do not use vain repetitions.

- If you have received the baptism of the Holy Spirit, pray in the spirit. If you have not yet received the fullness of the Holy Spirit, talk to your small group leader and ask him to pray with you.

- Try to pray while you are listening to inspiring music. This will intensify your time with God.

- Fasting is intensified prayer. Try fasting for a whole day.

- If you are sleepy, try praying while walking or kneeling down.

- Pray in a loud voice. God does not hear the volume of our voice when we pray aloud, but it makes it easier to concentrate.
- Call on the name of Jesus. Say his name aloud crying from your heart. You will obtain deep things from God.

CHAPTER 7

A DEVOTIONAL TIME ALONE WITH GOD

In this lesson, you will learn:

- The importance of separating time each day to be alone with God;
- How to begin and maintain a time alone with God;
- How to overcome the obstacles to this daily discipline;
- What to do during your time alone with God;

We can only develop intimacy through relationship. If you want to know God and have intimacy with him, then you will have to have a relationship with him.

Our relationship with God, just as with any other person, needs four things in order to develop; time, communication, circumstances and attitude.

Time

If you want to know God, you need to invest time with him. The time spent with God will water your spiritual roots, strengthen your trunk and nourish your leaves.

Communication

Without communication, we cannot get to know each other, much less share any intimacy one with another. True communication involves speaking and hearing, not just speaking about facts and ideas but also expressing them. You need to know what is in God's heart and share what is in yours. God communicates with you through your spirit and the written Word; and you communicate with him through prayer.

Circumstances

We get to know each other by observing how we act in certain circumstances. By going through the circumstances and situations that arise, we can learn to relate to God so that he can deal with us. A daily time alone with God will help you to perceive that he is in control, and to see how he is working in your life, and how you are responding to him.

Attitudes

Our attitude towards relationship will determine if it is a priority for us or not. If I am not interested in someone, I will not invest time to be with that person. You need to have a positive attitude about your time alone with God. Ask the Holy Spirit to place the desire within you and cultivate the hunger to be with God. Then you will achieve intimacy with him.

Do you desire the enjoyment of intimacy with the Father? It is important to know that you will not feel this desire automatically. It is necessary to separate time each day to be alone with the Lord.

Naturally, this is not a rule or a law. God's love for you will not change just because you have not been able to separate this time, but a lack of time spent with God will compromise your intimacy with him. Without investing this time with God, you will have a hard time recognizing his voice and understanding his will. He will continue to be your loving Heavenly Father, but you will not experience his friendship and intimacy, simply because you have not related to him on a daily basis. For this reason, we want to teach you how to separate a time each day to be with him as your Father.

The importance of separating a time to be with God

Your time alone with God must be the highest priority in your life. There are various reasons for this:

The first reason is that God created you for the purpose of having fellowship with him. Why do you think that God has created you in his image? The answer is simply because we cannot have fellowship with other beings different from us. God wants to have fellowship with you, that is why he created you in his own image (Genesis 1:27, 28).

The second reason is that God desires fellowship with his people. God's Word says that he has called you to the fellowship of his Son Jesus Christ, our Lord (1 Corinthians 1:9).

The third reason is that spending time alone with God is the secret to obtaining spiritual power. The power that Jesus manifested was a result of the time that he spent with the Father. The word says, "He went out and departed to a solitary place; and there he prayed." (Mark 1:35)

The fourth reason is that you need to eat spiritual bread daily in order to maintain your spiritual health and life. Many Christians do not experience life because they do not separate sufficient time to be alone with God. Jesus said,

> *"Man shall not live by bread alone, but by every word that proceeds from the mouth of God" (Matthew 4:4).*

Do you eat every day or just occasionally? In the same way, we need to feed our spirit every day.

How to begin a time alone with God

Choose an appropriate time

You can choose time to be alone with God at any time of day, but the Bible instructs us and experience shows that the morning is the best time. There are many reasons for this:

- David was a man after God's own heart and we know that he prayed in the morning.

  Cause me to hear your loving-kindness in the morning. For in you do I trust; cause me to know the way in which I should walk, for I lift up my soul to you. (Psalm 143:8)

- Jesus separated this time to be with God. In Mark 1:35 we read, Now in the morning, having risen a long while before daylight, he went out and departed to a solitary place; and there he prayed.

- We all know that the best time to tune a musical instrument is before the concert and not afterward. In your time alone with God, you prepare to face a new day.

- It shows that God has priority in your life. It shows that you prefer to spend time with God than do any other thing.

- You give God the best part of your day.

- You are most calm early in the morning, you tend to have less on your mind and your body has had its rest. This allows you to receive more from the Lord.

An appropriate amount of time

This is an example in of when quality is more important than quantity. However, little by little, try to increase the amount of time that you spend with God.

- Start with 15 minutes and increase progressively.
- Do not keep looking at your watch.
- Remember: spending time with the Lord is not just an obligation, but also a privilege.

An adequate location

Jesus had a habit it of praying on the Mount of Olives. In Luke 22:39 we read,

> *"Coming out, he went to the Mount of Olives, as he was accustomed, and his disciples also followed him."*

Find a place where you can have some privacy and where people will not interrupt you.

How to overcome obstacles

Two enemies will rise up and try to prevent you from spending time with God: your body and the devil.

The first enemy is your body. To overcome it, develop the following attitudes:

- Go to bed earlier. If you go to bed too late, you will unavoidably have a hard time waking up early, and if you do wake up earlier, you will be too sleepy. Use an alarm clock if necessary.
- Do not spend your time with God laying down (unless of course you are sick).
- Be careful with distractions
- Read the Bible and pray aloud. This will help you to maintain your concentration and take away the sleepiness.
- Overcome the tendency to be stuck in a rut by sharing with others what you have received from God in your time alone with him. The more you share with others, the more motivated you will be to continue.

The second enemy to overcome is the devil. He will try to use all kinds of things to distract your mind during your time alone with God. Therefore, be on your guard against him.

- Reject negative thoughts that your time with God is not being profitable. Such thoughts come from the evil one.

- Do not allow un-confessed, conscious sin to remain in your life. Un-confessed, conscious sin supplies a legal basis upon which the enemy can resist you.

- Do not spend this time in a hurry. Haste is a sign that the enemy has succeeded in entangling you with the concerns of daily life.

The last tactic that the enemy will use against you is to try to undermine your perseverance and your faithfulness in this discipline. This is the biggest problem. The best way to overcome it is to make a promise to God to continue no matter what and ask someone from your small group to keep you accountable for your daily time with God.

What to do during your time alone with God

Above all, remember that the objective of this time is not to study about Jesus, but to enjoy him. It does no good to know everything about an orange, like its color, chemical composition, nutritional value, methods of planting and reaping and yet never taste it. Knowing everything about oranges will not fill you with vitamin C, but if you drink orange juice, you will swallow the vitamin and reap its benefits. More important than learning about Jesus is to taste the life that he gives when he is in your life each day. You receive the benefits of the life of Christ through prayer, praise and worship, time in the Word and through several other spiritual disciplines.

Every man of God agrees that a time alone with God should have the following parts: confession, gratefulness, worship, intercession, petition and the reading of the Word. This is only a suggestion, not a rule; you can change both the sequence and the content according to the day and the circumstances.

Confess your sins

Be calm and reflective. Relax! Prepare your heart to hear the Lord. Breathe deeply a few times and wait on God. The Holy Spirit may convict you of some sin. Confess your sin and the peace of God will fill your heart. We need to begin with confession in order to come before the Lord with a pure heart.

Remember:

> If we confess our sins, he is faithful and just to forgive us our sins and cleanse us from all unrighteousness. (1 John 1:9).

Thank God

The word of God says:

> In everything give thanks, for this is the will of God in Christ Jesus. (1 Thessalonians 5:18)

This means that we should be grateful to God for everything that we have, and believe that whatever happens to us will result in blessing in the end. Giving thanks even if we do not feel the desire is not hypocrisy, but obedience. Never neglect the giving of thanks.

Some practical advice:

- Make a list of everything that God has done in your life and give him thanks;
- Be very specific. Develop a grateful heart before God. This will bring you satisfaction and enjoyment;
- Do not complain about anything but rather give thanks.

> Enter into his gates with thanksgiving, And into his courts with praise. Be thankful to him, and bless his name. (Psalm 100:4)

> Be anxious for nothing, but in everything by prayer and supplication, with thanksgiving, let your requests be made known to God; (Philippians 4:6)

Praise and worship the Lord

We should praise the Lord for everything that he is. God's Word says a lot about praise. The Psalms, the biggest book of the Bible, is composed entirely of praise to God. For us, the children of God, it is a pleasure and a privilege to worship him.

> Praise the Lord! Praise the Lord, O my soul! While I live I

will praise the Lord; I will sing praises to my God while I have my being. (Psalm 146:1- 2)

From the rising of the sun to its going down The Lord's name is to be praised. (Psalm 113:3)

Some practical advice for this time with God

- Declare what the Lord has done in your life and praise him for it;
- Sing some well-known praise songs;
- Use the book of Psalms as a worship guide, confessing verses that exalt God in a loud audible voice;
- Shout Hallelujah and glory to God. This will warm up your spirit;
- Learn how to play a musical instrument. This will increase your pleasure in the worship of God;
- Try using a worship CD during your time with God;
- The Bible describes the character of God in various forms. Make a personal list of these attributes. This is a way of getting to know God.

God's Character traits

TRAITS	MEANING	REFERENCE
Love	God loves you unconditionally.	1 John 3:16
Faithful	God will do everything that he has promised.	2 Corinthians 1:20
Holy	God is above everything and everyone.	Psalm 22:3; Revelation 15:4
Just	God is just in everything that he does.	2 Timothy 4:8
Good	God takes care of you.	Mk 10:18; Psalm 145:9
Wise	God transforms calamity into blessing.	Romans 11:33
Merciful	God does not treat you the way you deserve.	Lamentations 3:22 - 23
Omnipotent	There's nothing impossible for God	Luke 1:37; 18:27
Omniscient	God knows all things.	Psalm 33:13;139:1-4
Omnipresent	God is always with you	Psalm 139:7- 10
Unchangeable	God is the same yesterday, today and forever.	Mal. 3:6; Hebrews 13:8
Sovereign	God is in control of everything.	Revelation 19:6; Daniel 4:35

Intercession

To intercede is to pray for others and for God to meet their needs. To fail to intercede for those who are close to us, like friends and family, is sin before God.

> *Moreover, as for me, far be it from me that I should sin against the Lord in ceasing to pray for you; but I will teach you the good and the right way. (1 Samuel 12:23)*

- Make a list of the people that God has placed in your heart;
- Keep a list of the goals in prayer of your church;
- Pray for your small group;
- Pray for your fellow students and your fellow workers.

Intercessory Prayer list	
For my family	
For my friends	
For friends that I want to become Christians	
For my small group and for the Vine	
Others	

Petition/supplication

God wants to answer your prayers. Jesus said that whoever asks receives (Matthew 7:8). Besides this, he wants your joy to be full so it is in his interest to answer our requests.

> *Until now you have asked nothing in my name. Ask, and you will receive, that your joy may be full. (John 16:24)*

Here are some suggestions in order to pray more effectively:

- Develop a clear image of what you want and then express it in objective words. Clearly define what you want to receive from

God;

- We should offer all prayer in accordance with God's will as revealed in his Word. Search for texts in the Bible that refer to what you desire;
- Make your request to God in a simple and clear manner, according to what he has promised in his Word;
- Firmly believe that God has answered your request and that the answer is on its way;
- Reject all doubt that comes into your mind concerning what God has already answered in response to your prayer;
- Praise the Lord until the full manifestation of the answer to your request comes.

Bible reading

God's Word is the channel that God uses most to communicate with us, of course, he can speak in other ways, but the Bible is the most important one.

We will study this in more detail in further lessons, but for now, you need to understand how important the Bible is for you as a Christian.

> *All Scripture is given by inspiration of God, and is profitable for doctrine, for reproof, for correction, for instruction in righteousness, that the man of God may be complete, thoroughly equipped for every good work. (2 Timothy 3:16, 17)*

In 2 Timothy 3:16, 17 we read that God's Word is useful for the following reasons:

- Teaching or doctrine – it tells us what to believe;
- Rebuke – it shows us where we have erred;
- Correction – it helps us to return to the correct pattern;
- Teaching – it gives us direction and orientation for our life, so that we do not stumble.

In your time alone with God, the priority is to hear him and feel his word burning in your heart. Allow the Word to speak personally to you.

Points to ponder

- Try to go to sleep earlier so that you can be more alert during your time alone with God;

- Choose a tranquil place;

- Don't be hurried in your prayer time or in your Bible reading;

- Define clear objectives in prayer;

- Use a worship CD to inspire you in your time alone with God;

- Do not be afraid of silence. Be quiet before God and give him the opportunity to speak softly to your heart;

- Asked for someone from your small group to keep you accountable every day in your time alone with God;

- Be consistent;

- Don't change the time each day;

- Make your time with God your greatest priority; every three or four weeks, evaluate the development of your relationship with God together with your guardian angel;

- Use this book as a prayer guide to help you remember each part of prayer.

CHAPTER 8

FEEDING ON THE WORD AS SPIRITUAL FOOD

In this lesson, you will learn:

- The importance of God's Word in the Christian's life;
- The power of God's Word;
- How to feed daily on God's Word;

Everything that God does he does through his Word. God created everything that exists through his Word. Whenever you take in the living Word of God, something that formerly did not exist comes into existence. This is the marvel of the creative word.

Never say that you are weak, because the more that you confess weakness, the weaker you will become. However, if you believe on the Scriptures and declare that you are strong according to God's Word, then you will see the manifestation of his power. If you have any infirmity, do not accept it passively but look to God's Word that says, *"By his wounds we have been healed"* (Isa 53:5). Because of these words, you can declare that you are a healthy person.

We can trust completely on the faithfulness of God. If he has spoken, he will fulfill his words, because he cannot lie (Numbers 23:19; Hebrews 6:18)

God is "one" with his Word

When the Word proceeds from the mouth of God and we recognize it, we are receiving God himself inside of us.

If God and his Word are one, then I can know God by knowing his Word. To love God is to love his Word, to believe in God is to believe in his Word, to know God is to know his Word. In John, we read:

> *He who has My commandments and keeps them, it is he who loves Me. And he who loves Me will be loved by My Father, and I will love him and manifest Myself to him.*

(John 14:21)

Never forget that God and his Word are inseparable. Whoever loves God also Loves his Word. If God and his Word are one, then, I fill myself with God as I fill myself with his Word. In Ephesians, we find the biblical command:

> *And do not be drunk with wine, in which is dissipation; but*
> *be filled with the Spirit, speaking to one another in psalms*
> *and hymns and spiritual songs, singing and making melody*
> *in your heart to the Lord. (Ephesians 5:18, 19)*

Here we find the biblical way of being filled with God by his Spirit: by speaking. This is not just any speaking, but a spiritual speaking. We can say that the filling of the Spirit occurs by a speaking forth God's Word.

The Word engenders faith

> *So then faith comes by hearing, and hearing by the word of*
> *God. (Romans 10:17)*

We do not need to ask God for faith, we only need to hear his Word, confess it and practice it, and then faith manifests itself naturally.

Faith is merely practicing God's Word. To exercise faith is to act on the level that God has commanded, not only in relation to obeying the commandments of God, but in relation to acting in accordance with what God's Word teaches.

For example, if the Word says that God has seated me with Christ in the heavenly places, above all principalities and powers, then this is the position in which I must see myself and then I must act in accordance with this truth. This is what it means to practice the Word. If a demon appears before me, based on this word, I will say I am above you, because I am in Christ, seated in the heavenly places.

No matter what the problem is, God's Word has something to say about it. Find out what it says and act on it.

The Word engenders life

> *In the beginning was the Word, and the Word was with*
> *God, and the Word was God. He was in the beginning with*

God. All things were made through him, and without him nothing was made that was made. In him was life, and the life was the light of men (John 1:1-4)

God's Word brings life into our spirit. In John 6:63, Jesus said that his words are spirit and life. God re-created us in our spirit through God's Word. In his letter, James says:

Of his own will he brought us forth by the word of truth, that we might be a kind of firstfruits of his creatures. (James 1:18)

We were born by the Word of Truth. The new birth occurs through the Word. In Luke 8:11, we read that the word is a seed. Each seed bears fruit according to its kind. Apple seeds bear apple trees, dog seeds beget dogs and God's seed begets children of God.

Having been born again, not of corruptible seed but incorruptible, through the word of God which lives and abides forever, (1 Peter 1:23)

Whoever has been born of God does not sin, for his seed remains in him; and he cannot sin, because he has been born of God. (1 John 3:9)

The reason why we cannot live in the practice of sin is that inside of us the seed of God remains, which is his Word.

The Word is a spiritual weapon

And take the helmet of salvation, and the sword of the Spirit, which is the word of God; (Ephesians 6:17)

He had in his right hand seven stars, out of his mouth went a sharp two-edged sword, and his countenance was like the sun shining in its strength. (Revelation 1:16)

Then Jesus was led up by the Spirit into the wilderness to be tempted by the devil. And when he had fasted forty days and forty nights, afterward he was hungry. Now when the tempter came to him, he said, "If You are the Son of God, command that these stones become bread." But he answered and said, "It is written, 'Man shall not live by bread alone, but by every word that proceeds from the mouth of God.' "Then the devil took him up into the holy city, set him on the pinnacle of the temple, and said to him, "If You are the Son of God, throw Yourself down. For it is written: ' he shall give his angels charge over you,' and, 'In their hands they shall bear you up, Lest you dash your foot against a stone.' "Jesus said to him, "It is written again, 'You shall not tempt the LORD your God.'" Again, the devil took him up on an exceedingly high mountain, and showed him all the kingdoms of the world and their glory. And he said to him, "All these things I will give You if You will fall down and worship me." Then Jesus said to him, "Away with you, Satan! For it is written, 'You shall worship the LORD your God, and him only you shall serve.'" Then the devil left him, and behold, angels came and ministered to him. (Matthew 4:1-11)

And they overcame him by the blood of the Lamb and by the word of their testimony, and they did not love their lives to the death. (Revelation 12:11)

You are in a spiritual war. Your weapon is the Word of God, and it does not work in your hand but in your mouth.

Jesus left us his example of how to use God's Word against the Devil in Matthew 4. He had been fasting in the desert for forty days and, at the end, Satan came to tempt him. What did he do? He said, "*It is written*". He simply declared what was in the Scriptures. We must attack the enemy with the same weapon that Jesus used: the Word of God. Jesus knew the power of the Word in his mouth both to attack the enemy and to defend himself.

In Revelation we read:

And they overcame him by the blood of the Lamb and by the word of their testimony, and they did not love their lives to the death. (Revelation 12:11)

Your own strength is insufficient to defeat the devil; you need the power of God's Word.

Remember, God's Word is truth. The truth is not what you see, or what you feel, the truth is what God's Word says. Even though you do not see it, or feel it, even so, confess the Word with all of your heart.

Confession will birth faith in your spirit and produce the reality and experience of what God's Word says.

Declare who God is, what he does and what he has according to what he says in the Scriptures. Confess that you are what God says that you are, that you have what he says you have, and that you can do what he says you can do. Soon you will reap tremendous results.

The Word is spiritual bread

Jesus said:

> *Man shall not live by bread alone, but by every word that proceeds from the mouth of God. (Matthew 4:4)*

Every word that proceeds from the mouth of God is spiritual food for our nourishment. This food nourishes your spirit.

When a baby is born, its greatest need is to drink milk. Without food, the newborn will not only stop growing, but also will soon get weak and die. After we are saved and are born again, our greatest immediate need is to learn how to feed ourselves on the Lord, with the spiritual milk of the Word. Without this spiritual food, we will not grow normally and in a short time, we will die spiritually.

In 1 Peter, we read:

> *As newborn babes, desire the pure milk of the word, that you may grow thereby, if indeed you have tasted that the Lord is gracious. (1 Peter 2:2, 3)*

These verses clearly show how to take in the life of the Lord: drinking the genuine milk of the Word. If you want to experience Christ, you must drink the milk of the Word. In this way, your spirit will receive nourishment for spiritual growth. The Lord feeds his children through his Word. If you want to delight yourself in the Lord and feed upon him, you need to come to the Word.

You should not read the Bible only to learn and understand. In 2 Corinthians 3:6, we read that the "letter kills". Therefore, never take the Word of God as merely a book of knowledge or information, but as a book of life.

Whenever you read the Bible, you should appropriate something from God within yourself, just as when you eat material food. Just as food is assimilated into your body, your spirit will absorb the essence of the Word. We feed our spirit by eating words of faith (1 Timothy 4:6). God's Word is food for the nourishment of his children.

Jeremiah said, *"Your words were found, and I ate them,"* (15:16). Eating is not merely swallowing food, but absorbing it, digesting it and making it part of the body.

"And Your word was to me the joy and rejoicing of my heart;" (Jeremiah 15:16). After we take it in, the Word becomes joy and rejoicing. David said *"How sweet are Your words to my taste, Sweeter than honey to my mouth!"*(Psalm 119:103). The truth is that the Word satisfies us, becoming sweeter and tastier than honey to our lips.

Jesus said, in John 6:63 that his words were spirit and life. We know that *"God is Spirit"*. (John 4:24) Then the essence of God's Word is Spirit. The nature of the Scriptures is the essence of God himself. Every time that you approach God's Word, you should know that you are touching God himself.

The Word transforms

James 1:21 days that God's Word planted in us is powerful to save our souls. The salvation of the spirit has already happened; it is what we call the new birth. However, salvation on the level of the soul is a process that we call transformation. This transformation occurs by the Word that is sown within us.

Jesus said, in Mark 4:26-29, that the kingdom of God is like a man that sowed seed on the earth. The seed is the word and the earth is the heart. This man sleeps and then gets up, night and day until, without knowing how, and without trying, the seed germinates and grows. The same happens to us: all we need to do is sow the seed in the heart and it will germinate on its own in our life transforming us.

Paul said in Romans 12:2 that we must be transformed by the renewing of our minds. So how can we renew our minds? The answer is through God's Word. We must feed on the Word until our mind is renewed. The old patterns of thought and opinion should be conformed, or rather put in the form of the Word. Your life can only be transformed by God's Word and by the Holy Spirit.

Exchange your words for God's Word

For the word of God is living and powerful, and sharper

than any two-edged sword, piercing even to the division of soul and spirit, and of joints and marrow, and is a discerner of the thoughts and intents of the heart. (Hebrews 4:12)

God's Word is trustworthy and incorruptible. All things may pass away, but the Word will remain forever. The Holy Scriptures are not a mere book. Behind the printed words on the pages, is a person, God himself. Therefore, do not think of it in terms of paper and ink. Think about what God has said in his Word. The Word is an expression of God himself.

Many times, we tend to analyze circumstances and our own experiences according to our feeling or thoughts, abandoning that which God says about them.

Here are some examples:

The Word says, *"By his stripes, we were healed."* (Isaiah 53:5)

The believer says, "I am sick".

The Word says, *"In all these things, we are more than conquerors."* (Romans 8:37)

The believer says, "I am a failure".

The Word says, *"I can do all things through him that strengthens me."* (Philippians 4:17)

The believer says, "I am so weak, a miserable sinner. I am always falling."

Do you see the difference? You look at God's Word superficially, as if it were speaking of another person, and do not receive it as the truth. You do not see through the eyes of the Word, but through the eyes of your failure; then, you open your mouth and say things that are not in harmony with what God has said. Even worse, you say what Satan would like to see happen in your life. You must believe that God is true. You may feel crushed by your emotions, Satan may try to blind your eyes, but God is faithful. Have the courage to open your mouth and say "amen!" to everything that God has said.

God's Word is God himself speaking. God's Word is living, not some abstract object or concept. Jesus declared, "It is the Spirit who gives life; the flesh profits nothing. The words that I speak to you are spirit, and they are life" (John 6:53). The Word is living and produces life in the spirit, soul and body. It is the power of life, the seed of life, and the very life of God. This is the reason why a person is born again when he believes in Jesus, opens his mouth and confesses him as Lord. It is the Word producing life.

God's Word is living and active, perfect, efficient, powerful and capable. It transforms human nature, changes any situation and any circumstance.

> *For with God nothing is ever impossible and no word from*
> *God shall be without power or impossible of fulfillment.*
> *(Luke 1:37 Amplified version)*

This blessed Word is the basis of our faith. Our thoughts and feelings can never serve as the basis for our faith. The infallible Word of God should be the foundation of our faith. If we wish to know God, we will have to know his Word, since it expresses who he is. If we wish to know the will of God, we will need to know his Word, since it reveals his purposes for our lives. God has spoken in various ways, but the principal way is through his written Word.

As long as you walk on the ground of God's Word, you will have success. However, the moment that you leave this ground you will have entered on slippery ground and will be condemned to failure. Therefore, trust on the integrity of God's Word and allow it to be the foundation of your life. Remain steadfast upon the Word and refuse to abandon it. Discipline your mind and allow only words that line-up with God's Word to proceed from your lips.

Make it your goal to make a radical change in the words that you speak. Make the following audible confessions based on God's Word.

- Never again will I say, "I can't" for I can do all things through him that strengthens me. (Philippians 4:13)
- Never again will I say that I do not have enough, because my God shall supply all my need according to his riches in glory by Christ Jesus. (Philippians 4:19)
- Never again will I say that I am weak, because The LORD is the strength of my life, (Psalm 27:1) and the people who know their God shall be strong, and carry out great exploits. (Daniel 11:32)

- Never again will I say that I am afraid, because God has not given us a spirit of fear, but of power and of love and of a sound mind. (2 Timothy 1:7)

- Never again will I say that Satan rules over my life, because he who is in me is greater than he who is in the world. (1 John 4:4)

- Never again will I say that I am defeated, because God always leads me in triumph in Christ. (2 Corinthians 2:14)

- Never again will I say that I have no wisdom, because Christ Jesus became the wisdom of God for me. (1 Corinthians 1:30)

- Never again will I say that I am sick, because by his stripes I am healed (Isaiah 53:5), and he himself took my infirmities and bore my sicknesses. (Matthew 8:17)

- Never again will I say that I am worried and frustrated, because I can cast all my care upon him, for he cares for me. (1 Peter 5:7)

- Never again will I say that I am imprisoned, because where the Spirit of the Lord is, there is liberty. (2 Corinthians 3:17)

- Never again will I say that I am condemned, because there is no condemnation to those who are in Christ Jesus. Therefore, I am free of all condemnation. (Romans 8:1)

CHAPTER 9

HOW TO STUDY THE WORD

In this lesson, you will learn:

- The importance of hearing God's Word;
- How to study and memorize the Word;
- How to meditate on the Word to receive its riches;

Non-Christians always associate believers with the Bible, which is good. Others however, say that it is just like deodorant for believers because they carry it under their arm, or use it as a kind of good luck charm, but they never actually read it. If you wish to grow in God, you must practice God's Word because . . .

> *All Scripture is given by inspiration of God, and is profitable for doctrine, for reproof, for correction, for instruction in righteousness, that the man of God may be complete, thoroughly equipped for every good work. (2 Timothy 3:16,17)*

However, for this to happen, you must have a heart knowledge of the Word, which happens in five ways:

- Hearing
- Reading
- Studying
- Memorizing
- Meditating

How to hear God's Word

We receive faith upon hearing God's Word:

> *Faith comes by hearing and hearing by the Word of God. Several times Jesus said: He who has ears to hear, let him*

hear! (Matthew 11:15)

Therefore, it is vital to hear God's Word. For this to happen you must participate in the weekly worship services of your local church because when you hear the Word, it engenders faith within you so that you can overcome the world and be able to serve God day by day.

There are various ways to hear the Word:

- Listen to it narrated on CD or mp3
- Sermons preached at your local church services
- Bible studies at the church building or in a small group
- Recorded sermons
- Radio or Television

The problem is that we only retain about 5 to 10% if what we hear. However, we can improve this statistic if we follow the tips below:

- Develop a hunger and desire to hear God. Develop a deep yearning to retain much more of what you hear.
- Open your heart and mind. A person with a closed, fearful and proud mind can hear, but cannot retain God's Word.
- Concentrate on hearing. Do not allow daily and routine concerns or occupations take away your attention from hearing the Word.
- Write down what you hear. Keep a notebook for notes on sermons. In Hebrews, we read:

  Therefore, we must give the more earnest heed to the things we have heard, lest we drift away. (Hebrews 2:1)

- Practice what you hear.

  But be doers of the word, and not hearers only, deceiving yourselves. (James 1:22)

How to read God's Word

When we hear the Word, we retain 5 to 10% of what we hear. However, we retain 30% of what we read.

The command of God is that you read the Word every day of your life. You must have a bible with you always.

*And it shall be with him, and he shall read it all the days of
his life, that he may learn to fear the LORD his God and be
careful to observe all the words of this law and these
statutes. (Deuteronomy 17:19)*

Deuteronomy 17:19 reveals three reasons for us to read the Word,
*that we learn to fear the LORD our God, keep all the words of this
law, and observe these statutes.*

Paul also exhorted Timothy saying:

*Till I come, give attention to reading, to exhortation, to
doctrine. (1 Tim. 4:13)*

John said that those who read and hear are blessed:

*Blessed is he who reads and those who hear the words of
this prophecy, and keep those things which are written in it;
for the time is near. (Revelation 1:3)*

Many believers have never read the Bible from Genesis to
Revelation. This shows the place that God's Word occupies in their
lives.

Here are some suggestions for reading and retaining God's Word:

- If you read three chapters per day and four on Sundays, you
  will have read the whole Bible in one year.

- Read systematically.

- Get your own bible and underline the verses that speak the
  most to you.

- Read in a quiet place where you can concentrate.

- Get a Bible-reading plan and follow it. At the end of this
  chapter, there is a suggested bible-reading plan.

How to study God's Word

If you want to retain more of God's Word, you will need to study it.
If you do this, you will retain from 30 to 50% of everything that you
study.

Many people however, get anxious when they hear the word study.
Do not worry; I am not talking about taking a theological seminary
course or anything like that. You will see that there are very simple

ways of studying the Bible.

God's Word says that noble people study and examine the scriptures, but foolish people just listen to it.

These were more fair-minded than those in Thessalonica, in that they received the word with all readiness, and searched the Scriptures daily to find out whether these things were so. (Acts 17:11)

In addition, the objective of studying the Word is so that you can "Be diligent to present yourself approved to God, a worker who does not need to be ashamed, rightly dividing the word of truth." (2 Timothy 2:15)

George Muller, a great man of God, developed some questions that he used in his own study of the Word. They will help you to better understand what God is saying through his Word.

When you are studying, you can analyze the text in question asking yourself all of these questions:

- Is there an example for me to follow?
- Is there a commandment for me to obey?
- Is there a mistake that I can avoid?
- Is there a sin of which I should confess and repent?
- Is there a thought about God's nature?
- Is there a promise that I can claim?

After asking these questions, you may still have doubts. In this case, a good alternative is to purchase good books that help you understand God's Word.

Ask your leader or discipler to help you buy some.

How to memorize God's Word

Eventually you will end up spontaneously memorizing several Bible verses simply because of the fact that you will hear them repeatedly in church services. However, God's will is that you make the memorization of Bible verses a constant part of your life. God commands us to memorize the Word in Deuteronomy 11:18:

Therefore you shall lay up these words of mine in your

heart and in your soul, and bind them as a sign on your hand, and they shall be as frontlets between your eyes. And you shall write them on the doorposts of your house and on your gates, (Deuteronomy 11:18, 20)

When we hide God's Word in our heart, the Lord keeps us from sin.

Your word I have hidden in my heart, That I might not sin against You. (Psalm 119:11)

The great value of memorization is that we retain 100% of what we memorize. When you fill your mind with God's Word, your way of thinking begins to change. No one falls into sin if his or her mind is full of God's Word.

The law of his God is in his heart; None of his steps shall slide. (Psalm 37:31)

Tips to help memorize scripture:

- Take advantage of the times that you are inactive or waiting for someone like at a doctor's office or in a line at the bank or post office.
- Choose a verse that speaks to your heart
- Write the verse down on an index card or put it on your phone or iPad
- Repeat it, reading it aloud many times
- Divide the verse into complete phrases
- Carry the verse with you for review
- Always memorize the verse just as it is written
- As you memorize the verse erase or delete the part that you have already committed to memory
- If there is a song whose words correspond to the verse that you are memorizing take advantage of it.

How to meditate on God's Word

In Psalm 1:2, we read that the blessed *"takes his delight is in the law of the LORD, And in his law he meditates day and night."* Therefore:

He shall be like a tree Planted by the rivers of water, That brings forth its fruit in its season, Whose leaf also shall not wither; And whatever he does shall prosper. (Psalm 1:3)

God also commanded Joshua:

This Book of the Law shall not depart from your mouth, but you shall meditate in it day and night, that you may observe to do according to all that is written in it. For then you will make your way prosperous, and then you will have good success. (Joshua 1:8)

God invites you to meditate on his Law at all times, day and night. However, what does it mean to meditate? Meditation is not emptying your mind of all thoughts, like the oriental religions teach.

Meditation is a prolonged thinking directed to a single objective. The Bible illustrates this practice by referring to animals that chew the cud. After swallowing the food, they regurgitate the chewed up cud, and thus extract the greatest amount of nutrients possible from the food.

In practice, meditating involves four aspects: visualization, personalization, application and confession.

Visualization

When you read or hear a story without using your imagination to visualize it, you do not feel the emotions that are involved. The same applies to God's Word. Meditation is visualizing, imagining what is going on in the passage that you are reading. In Psalm 23, you read the words: *"The Lord is my shepherd"*. This can seem dry and uninteresting, without imagining a helpless lamb in the protective hands of a shepherd. The image of the imagination inspired by the words is what builds faith.

Personalization

To personalize the Bible text is to place it in the first person, to re-tell the story as if you were the main character. The majority of Bible texts can be personalized. In Psalm 91, for example, we read *"He who dwells in the secret place of the Most High Shall abide under the shadow of the Almighty."* Personalizing this text, you can say, "Since I dwell in the secret place of the Most High, I will abide under the shadow of the Almighty.

Application

Every Bible text has a single meaning, but innumerable applications. Always consider it as a Word of God directed to your life.

Confession

Every Bible text can be used as a prayer. Using your own words, repeat the text that you have just read as a prayer to God. This word will definitively be carved into your heart and the Holy Spirit will bring it to your mind whenever you need it.

In Hebrews 12:1, we read, "*let us run with endurance the race that is set before us*". The Christian life is like a race. Imagine that you are participating in this race on a lightweight bicycle. You can remember the five elements of a good quiet time as if they were spokes on the wheel of a bicycle that we can call the wheel of prayer. The five spokes of this wheel are confession, gratitude, worship, intercession and petition. We can call the front wheel the wheel of God's Word with five spokes: hear, read, study, memorize and meditate.

MEMORY VERSE GUIDE

This group of memory verses makes up the structure of the fundamentals of the Christian life. These verses can also help you evangelize your friends. Every Christian should know all of these verses by heart.

Your new Life

Christ is the center	2 Corinthians 5:17; Galatians 2:20
Obedience to Christ	Romans 12:1; John 14:21
God's Word	1 Timothy 3:16; Joshua 1:8
Prayer	John 15:7; Philippians 4:6-7
Fellowship	Matthew 18:20; Hebrews 10:24
Testimony	Matthew 4:19; Romans 1:16

The Testimony of Christ

All men are sinners	Romans 3:23; 2:12
The wages of sin	Romans 6:23; Hebrews 9:27
Christ paid the price	Romans 5:8; 1 Peter 3:18
Salvation not by works	Ephesians 2:8,9; Titus 3:5
All must receive Christ	John 1:12; Revelation 3:20
Assurance of salvation	1 John 5:13; John 5:24

God's resources for us

His Spirit	1 Corinthians 3:16; 2:12
His strength	Isaiah 41:10; Philippians 4:13
His Faithfulness	Lamentations 3:22; Num. 23:19
His Peace	Isaiah 26:3; 1 Peter 5:7
His Provision	Romans 8:32; Philippians 4:19
His Help in Temptation	Hebrews 2:18; Psalm 119:9,11

The disciple of Christ

Jesus in first place	Matthew 6:33; Luke 9:23
Separate from the World	1 John 2:15, 16; Romans 2:12
Steadfast	1 Corinthians 15:58; Hebrews 12:3
Serves others	Mark 10:45; 2 Corinthians 4:5
Gives Generously	Proverbs 3:9-10; 2 Corinthians 9:6,7
Preaches the Gospel	Acts 1:8; Matthew 28:19-20

BIBLE READING PLAN
THE NEW TESTAMENT IN 30 DAYS

Day	Book	Chap	Eval	Day	Book	Chap	Eval
1	Matt	1-9		16	Acts	15-21	
2	Matt	10-15		17	Acts	22-28	
3	Matt	16-22		18	Rom	1-8	
4	Matt	23-28		19	Rom	9-16	
5	Mark	1-8		20	1 Cor.	1-9	
6	Mark	9-16		21	1 Cor.	10-16	
7	Luke	1-6		22	2 Cor.	1-13	
8	Luke	7-11		23	Gal. & Eph.		
9	Luke	12-18		24	Phil., 1 &2 Tess.		
10	Luke	19-24		25	1,2 Tim. & Phil.		
11	John	1-7		26	Hebrews		
12	John	8-13		27	James, 1 & 2 Pet.		
13	John	14-22		28	1,2,&3 John		
14	Acts	1-7		29	Rev	1-11	
15	Acts	8-14		30	Rev	12-22	

CHAPTER 10

LEARN TO BELIEVE

In this lesson, you will learn:

- What faith is and what types of faith exist
- How faith can be obtained
- Tips on how to exercise your faith

What is faith? God's Word says that "faith" is the substance of things hoped for, the evidence of things not seen. (Hebrews 11:1) Biblical faith proceeds from the heart and not the mind. A mere rational agreement is not enough, it is necessary to apply the heart in order to believe on God's Word. The faith that begins in the heart has the power to remove mountains. Jesus said:

> *For assuredly, I say to you, whoever says to this mountain, 'Be removed and be cast into the sea,' and does not doubt in his heart, but believes that those things he says will be done, he will have whatever he says. (Mark 11:23)*

You can be like Abraham:

> *(As it is written, "I have made you a father of many nations") in the presence of him whom he believed - God, who gives life to the dead and calls those things which do not exist as though they did; who, contrary to hope, in hope believed, so that he became the father of many nations, according to what was spoken, "So shall your descendants be." And not being weak in faith, he did not consider his own body, already dead (since he was about a hundred years old), and the deadness of Sarah's womb. He did not waver at the promise of God through unbelief, but was strengthened in faith, giving glory to God, and being fully convinced that what he had promised he was also able to perform. (Romans 4:17-21)*

Abraham's faith persevered against all evidence. Everything around him appeared contrary to God's promises, but he persevered in believing and saw the fulfillment of God's promise.

You can also have faith like Thomas, one of the twelve who was not with the other disciples when Jesus appeared.

> *The other disciples therefore said to him, "We have seen the Lord." So he said to them, "Unless I see in his hands the print of the nails, and put my finger into the print of the nails, and put my hand into his side, I will not believe." And after eight days his disciples were again inside, and Thomas with them. Jesus came, the doors being shut, and stood in the midst, and said, "Peace to you!" Then he said to Thomas, "Reach your finger here, and look at My hands; and reach your hand here, and put it into My side. Do not be unbelieving, but believing." And Thomas answered and said to him, "My Lord and my God!" Jesus said to him, "Thomas, because you have seen Me, you have believed. Blessed are those who have not seen and yet have believed." (John 20:25-29)*

Thomas based his faith on what he saw. Jesus seriously rebuked him for harboring such an attitude. Do not wait to see in order to believe later. Such faith is useless and has no value to God. However if you believe, you will bring into the material and visible world what is already a reality in the invisible world of faith and God's promises.

Types of faith in God's Word

Saving faith

Each person receives a sufficient measure of faith to believe for his or her own salvation. Without this measure of faith, no one could ever receive salvation. In Ephesians, the apostle Paul wrote:

> *For by grace you have been saved through faith, and that not of yourselves; it is the gift of God, not of works, lest anyone should boast. (Ephesians 2:8, 9)*

Sanctifying faith

After conversion, you receive a new measure of faith.

> *For I say, through the grace given to me, to everyone who*

is among you, not to think of himself more highly than he ought to think, but to think soberly, as God has dealt to each one a measure of faith. (Romans 12:3)

This measure of faith will enable you to live the Christian life just as God has planned: in victory. You can and must develop your faith because if you do not exercise it, you will not receive anything from God.

The Gift of faith

Not all Christians possess the third type of faith. It is a spiritual gift.

For to one is given the word of wisdom through the Spirit, to another the word of knowledge through the same Spirit, to another faith by the same Spirit, to another gifts of healings by the same Spirit, (1 Corinthians 12:8, 9)

The gift of faith releases the resurrection of the dead and the manifestation of great signs of God. Such miracles can only be accomplished through the gift of faith.

The difference between faith and hope

Most people confuse faith with hope. However, they are quite different from each other as we will see in 1 Corinthians 13:13

And now abide faith, hope, love, these three; but the greatest of these is love.

Faith acts in the present and hope deals with the future. To have faith is simply to affirm that what God says in his Word is the truth, declaring that the things that we are seeking already exist. To have hope is to project into the future what we yearn for today. The things for which the Bible teaches us to wait do not depend on our faith. For example, whether we believe in the return of Jesus or not, he will return; therefore we wait for him. On the other hand, the things that depend upon faith only happen if we exercise faith. Jesus said:

Therefore I say to you, whatever things you ask when you pray, believe that you receive them, and you will have them. (Mark 11:24)

He did not say believe and receive, or wait and receive, but believe that you have received. The verb is in the past tense. For him who believes, the promise is already a reality, and not a thing that we wait for.

How can we obtain faith?

We have seen that every believer has already received a measure of faith. However, in order to develop it, we must exercise it. God can grant us faith in three different ways. We receive faith by:

Hearing God's Word

In Romans 10:7 we read, *"So then faith comes by hearing, and hearing by the word of God."*

Praying in the spirit

Paul explained, in 1 Corinthians 14:14, that *"if I pray in a tongue, my spirit prays, but my understanding is unfruitful."* Therefore, we learn that at least one way of praying in the spirit is by praying in tongues.

Jude (1:20) says *"But you, beloved, building yourselves up on your most holy faith, praying in the Holy Spirit,"* Therefore, as you invest time praying in the spirit; your faith will be tremendously edified.

Seeing the result of faith

There is a normal sequence for the manifestation of faith. We can see an occurrence of this sequence when Peter asked the Lord to command him to come to him on the water, in Matthew 14:28-31:

> *And Peter answered him and said, Lord, if it is You, command me to come to You on the water. So he said, "Come." And when Peter had come down out of the boat, he walked on the water to go to Jesus. But when he saw that the wind was boisterous, he was afraid; and beginning to sink he cried out, saying, "Lord, save me!" And immediately Jesus stretched out his hand and caught him, and said to him, "O you of little faith, why did you doubt?"*

In this sequence, you can clearly see the equation of victory. First Peter heard the Word, then he believed on the Word, and finally, he obeyed the Word. The result of this equation is faith and victory. Because of this, Peter was able to walk on the water; however, he soon began to sink. He lost his faith. Why did this happen? Peter initiated another sequence, composed of the equation of unbelief: he looked at the circumstances; which caused him to become afraid, then as a result of his fear, he doubted and the result was failure and defeat.

The equation of faith:

Hear the Word + believe in the Word + obey the Word = victory

The equation of unbelief:

Look and the circumstances + fear + doubt = failure

Tips on how to exercise your faith

- Look for a promise in the Bible related to what you want to see happen or wish to receive. It does no good to try to believe for something that God has not promised in his Word because only God's Word generates faith.

- Believe in God's Word. Simply consider how what you are seeking is a fulfillment of the promises of God, because he his faithful to fulfill everything that he has said that he would do.

- Refuse to consider contrary circumstances perceived through the physical senses.

- Praise the Lord for the answers

Confession of faith

According to the dictionary, to confess is to recognize, agree or admit, a fact, to declare faith in a thing. It can be confession of some fault or sin. You have already learned to confess your sins, but you still need to learn to confess God's Word.

Confession of God's Word is important for 3 reasons:

It produces faith.

It dissipates fear.

It appropriates promises. We can only have what we confess.
Jesus said:

> *"Therefore whoever confesses Me before men, him I will also confess before My Father who is in heaven. But whoever denies Me before men, him I will also deny before My Father who is in heaven. (Matthew 10:32, 33)*

In Romans 10:10, we read

"With the heart one believes unto righteousness, and with the mouth confession is made unto salvation."

In order to cast mountains into the sea we must speak to them. Jesus said:

Therefore consider the goodness and severity of God: on those who fell, severity; but toward you, goodness, if you continue in his goodness. Otherwise you also will be cut off. And they also, if they do not continue in unbelief, will be grafted in, for God is able to graft them in again. For if you were cut out of the olive tree which is wild by nature, and were grafted contrary to nature into a cultivated olive tree, how much more will these, who are natural branches, be grafted into their own olive tree? (Mark 11:22-24)

CHAPTER 11

LEARN TO GIVE

In this lesson, you will learn:
* What tithes and offerings are
* What you should give
* Why pay tithes to God
* How, when and where to pay tithes
* Tips for dealing with the matter of tithes in your life

Many people all over the world think that poverty is a virtue. It is common to think that poverty is a requisite for humility and that poverty draws us nearer to God, while riches always distance us from God. Many of us have been taught that it is wrong to ask God for money or property. Many Christians have a mentality that accepts poverty as a legitimate state in which God's people should live.

God's Word however, teaches that poverty is a curse. Poverty made its scene after the fall of man in the Garden of Eden. Conversely, riches and prosperity are blessings that God has reserved for all his children. Although poverty is clothed in the appearance of humility, it is a curse sent to keep you away from the blessings of God.

Now that you have come to the kingdom of God, all curses are broken and God's promise may come to you.

> *If you are willing and obedient, You shall eat the good of the land; (Isaiah 1:19)*

The promise is that the Lord is your shepherd and you will lack nothing (Psalm 23:1). No more eating well only once a week, no more wearing torn clothing and shoes with holes in them, no more sleeping on a broken box spring, no more paying late fees for unpaid bills and living in a rented house.

You are a child of God. Your Father is the owner of all provision and riches and he gave you the keys to the abundance and prosperity of his storehouse. God will not deny you any good thing, if you believe in his goodness and provision.

Some call God the Divine Eternal Father, it is true and you are his child. God takes pleasure in your prosperity because you are his child.

All of these promises are only for the children that consecrate themselves to God and surrender control of their lives to him. Therefore, Mammon, the god of this age, does not control them. Paying your tithe and giving offerings is the way that he established for us to be free from Mammon.

Why must I give offerings?

It causes me to resemble God

> *For God so loved the world that he gave his only begotten Son, that whoever believes in him should not perish but have everlasting life. (John 3:16)*

God expressed his love for us by giving his own Son. Following the same principle, giving is a way of expressing our love for him.

The act of giving directs my heart to God

Jesus said:

> *For where your treasure is, there your heart will be also. (Matthew 6:21)*

If our treasure is in God, then we will naturally direct our giving to him.

Giving honors God

> *Honor the LORD with your possessions, And with the firstfruits of all your increase; So your barns will be filled with plenty, And your vats will overflow with new wine. (Proverbs 3:9, 10)*

Giving is an investment

> *Give, and it will be given to you: good measure, pressed down, shaken together, and running over will be put into your bosom. For with the same measure that you use, it will be measured back to you." (Luke 6:38)*

Giving brings blessing

> *He who has a generous eye will be blessed, For he gives of his bread to the poor. (Proverbs 22:9)*

> *The generous soul will be made rich, And he who waters will also be watered himself. (Proverbs 11:25)*

It is better to give than to receive

> *I have shown you in every way, by laboring like this, that you must support the weak. And remember the words of the Lord Jesus, that he said, 'It is more blessed to give than to receive.'" (Acts 20:35)*

What the Bible teaches about tithes

The word tithe means a tenth part of something. Ten percent of everything that passes through our hands must be surrendered to the Lord, since the tithe is holy, separated for God's exclusive use. In Leviticus, we read:

> *And concerning the tithe of the herd or the flock, of whatever passes under the rod, the tenth one shall be holy to the LORD. (Leviticus 27:32)*

Tithes and offerings belong to God

When you do not pay your tithes, you are robbing God. If you steal from men, you will come under a curse. Just imagine what happens when you rob God!

> *"Will a man rob God? Yet you have robbed Me! But you say, 'In what way have we robbed You?' In tithes and offerings. You are cursed with a curse, For you have robbed Me, Even this whole nation. (Malachi 3:8, 9)*

The tithe is distinct from offerings

The tithe is ten percent of all income, but offerings are voluntary and go beyond the tithe. The tithe is for protection against the devourer, while the offering is for prosperity through sowing and reaping. In Malachi 3:11, we read that if we pay our tithes, the Lord will rebuke the devourer on our behalf. The tithe is law, and tests our faithfulness. Our offering however demonstrates the degree of our love and it should be more than our tithe.

The tithe is not a seed, but offerings are seeds. God's Word says that whoever sows bountifully, will also reap bountifully because God is faithful.

> *But this I say: He who sows sparingly will also reap sparingly, and he who sows bountifully will also reap bountifully. (2 Corinthians 9:6)*

Why should I pay a tithe?

Because God commands it

> *And all the tithe of the land, whether of the seed of the land or of the fruit of the tree, is the LORD's. It is holy to the LORD. (Luke 27:30)*

Because Jesus was a tither

> *Jesus came to fulfill the law therefore, he was a tither. According to his example, we should also be tithers.*

> *"Woe to you, scribes and Pharisees, hypocrites! For you pay tithe of mint and anise and cumin, and have neglected the weightier matters of the law: justice and mercy and faith. These you ought to have done, without leaving the others undone. (Matthew 23:23)*

The tithe reminds me that everything that I have belongs to God

> *"And you shall remember the LORD your God, for it is he who gives you power to get wealth, that he may establish his covenant which he swore to your fathers, as it is this day. (Deuteronomy 8:18)*

The tithe expresses my gratitude to God

> *Every man shall give as he is able, according to the blessing of the LORD your God which he has given you. (Deuteronomy 16:17)*

> *What shall I render to the LORD For all his benefits toward me? (Psalm 116:12)*

If I do not pay my tithe, I will be robbing God

> *"Will a man rob God? Yet you have robbed Me! But you say, 'In what way have we robbed You?' In tithes and*

offerings. You are cursed with a curse, For you have robbed Me, Even this whole nation. (Malachi 3:8, 9)

The tithe releases unlimited blessing from God

Bring all the tithes into the storehouse, That there may be food in My house, And try Me now in this," Says the LORD of hosts, "If I will not open for you the windows of heaven And pour out for you such blessing That there will not be room enough to receive it. (Malachi 3:10)

The tithe is a protection against the devil

"And I will rebuke the devourer for your sakes, So that he will not destroy the fruit of your ground, Nor shall the vine fail to bear fruit for you in the field," Says the LORD of hosts; (Mal. 3:11)

Helpful tips

- Do not hold on to your tithe. Put it in the collection plate or box during the first worship service after you receive your salary.

  On the first day of the week let each one of you lay something aside, storing up as he may prosper, that there be no collections when I come. (1 Corinthians 16:2)

- You can calculate your tithe based on the amount of your gross or net salary, but your gross salary is your true salary so you should tithe on everything.

- Nobody has the authority to administer his or her own tithe, or offerings we must bring them to Lord's house (the local church). Any other use is inspired of the evil one. Do not pay your tithe to prophets, evangelists or even to mission organizations. The destination must be the local church.

- We should bring all our tithes to the local church where we are cared for and spiritually fed. To pay your tithe to another church is like a married man spending his salary on another family instead of or in addition to his own. This is spiritual prostitution.

- God does not authorize any pastor or leader to relieve church members of their obligation to pay their tithes. No man can authorize anyone to disobey God's Word.

- Pay your tithes before paying any other bill. Whoever pays their bills before paying their tithe is sinning and shows that God is not a priority.

- We must calculate our tithe considering all of our income, including overtime, sale of goods or real estate, investments and gifts.

- Be organized. Keep track of all of your income, no matter the amount. This is the only way that you will be a faithful tither; otherwise, you will be at the mercy of the devourer.

- A business person can only be considered a faithful tither if he pays the tithe of his company's income and not only his salary.

- Nobody can determine what the church does with the tithes that it receives. Only the church leadership, pastors and elders administer tithes.

- Faithful tithers have the right to see monthly financial reports from the church. At the very least, the church should present an annual report of the church's finances.

- Nobody is exempt from paying tithes. All the pastors, missionaries; even those who are unemployed and receive financial help from the church should pay tithes on this income.

- God does not lend tithes to anyone. Whoever knows the truth and fails to pay the tithe is under a curse because it is the same as robbing God.

- If you failed to pay your tithe for several months, do not simply continue from where you left off, pay all the late tithes that you failed to deliver to the church.

- Obtain a tithe envelope and submit yourself to the normal protocol for paying your tithe. Write your name and amount each time you pay your tithe.

- Never come empty handed to any worship service. The bible commands us to be ready at all times to make an offering when we gather for a worship service. The time of offering and paying of tithes is an integral part of the worship service.

Three times a year all your males shall appear before the LORD your God in the place which he chooses: at the Feast of Unleavened Bread, at the Feast of Weeks, and at the Feast of Tabernacles; and they shall not appear before the LORD empty-handed." (Deuteronomy 16:16

- Do not make a show when giving an offering or paying a tithe in the worship service. If you seek recognition or glory of men, that will be your only reward.

CHAPTER 12

FELLOWSHIP IN THE FAMILY OF GOD

In this lesson, you will learn:

- The importance of maintaining ties to the local church fellowship
- What a cell group of the church is
- How to have fellowship with the saints

God never meant for us to live alone in isolation. Life in community is the biblical form of living the Christian life. The more that you grow in God and attain more intimacy with him, the closer you will feel drawn to others especially your brothers and sisters in the Lord.

Imagine a circle. Now imagine that God is in the middle of this circle and we are on the edges of it. You may be on one side of the circle and I may be on the other side but the closer we approach God, surprisingly the closer we approach each other. The only way to demonstrate our intimacy with God is through our fellowship with other Christians.

Why is fellowship so important?

The correctness of your theology is not the most important thing, nor are your extraordinary gifts or your ample strategic vision: if you are an individualist and have no fellowship with the church, you are outside of the will of God.

Without fellowship, you are a loose brick taken out of the wall, a body member cut off from the body, a lost soldier in battlefield, an incoherent contradiction and a life with no purpose. You need to relate to the local church for innumerable reasons:

You are part of the same family

The bible teaches that we are of the family of God:

Therefore, as we have opportunity, let us do good to all, especially to those who are of the household of faith. (Galatians 6:10)

Now, therefore, you are no longer strangers and foreigners, but fellow citizens with the saints and members of the household of God, (Ephesians 2:19)

You are united with your natural family members by much more than just living under the same roof. You have the same genetic make-up as the rest of your family members. The same applies to your spiritual family, which is the local church. We are a family not just, because we worship at the same address, but also because we share the same life that comes from Christ, having the same spiritual genetic make-up since we are all children of God. A dog cannot have fellowship with a cat, neither a rat with an elephant. They do not possess the same type of life. Since you are now light, you can no longer have fellowship with darkness. You are unable to maintain a close relationship of deep sharing with anyone who does not also possess God's life inside of them. For this type of companionship, you need a spiritual family.

You cannot grow by yourself

Just as a child learns from its parents and older siblings, you also need spiritual brothers and parents in order to grow and mature in God. If you neglect your need for a spiritual family, you will bring harm to your own spiritual life.

Some churches merely offer a place for their members to go when they have a need and are seeking some kind of blessing. It is not wrong to seek blessing but that is not what defines a church. Moreover, these types of activities do not lead to spiritual growth. There are occasions in which you need to be exhorted, corrected, motivated or encouraged, sometimes even carried, and many times forgiven.

In order to grow, you need to have a commitment and relationship with God and the only way this can happen is through his body, the Church.

Fellowship is a safeguard for you

It is not hard to imagine what happens to an ember taken out of the fire. Nor is it necessary to discuss the futility of going to war alone. Therefore, the fellowship within the church is a type of spiritual protection for you. Through fellowship, you maintain your spiritual fire and win the battle. We learn in Ecclesiastes that a threefold cord is not easily broken.

Two are better than one, Because they have a good reward for their labor. For if they fall, one will lift up his companion. But woe to him who is alone when he falls, For he has no one to help him up. Again, if two lie down together, they will keep warm; But how can one be warm alone? Though one may be overpowered by another, two can withstand him. And a threefold cord is not quickly broken. (Ecclesiastes 4:9-12)

Christ manifests himself through fellowship

Normally people express themselves through their own body. However, if in some way our body became paralyzed, then we would have no way of expressing ourselves or doing the things we want. The same principle applies to Christ and the Church. The Church is the body of Christ and it is through his body that he expresses himself. For this reason, he said, *"Wherever there are two or three people gathered in My name, I will be there also"* (Matthew 18:20). In one way, to be out of fellowship is to be far from the presence of the Lord.

There is power when we are together

Jesus said:

Again I say to you that if two of you agree on earth concerning anything that they ask, it will be done for them by My Father in heaven. (Matthew 18:19)

God will not answer certain prayers unless we pray together with someone, in agreement and fellowship. You can accomplish many things by yourself, but to accomplish the greatest and most important things you should always work with a team, either within the cell or through the whole church body.

Fellowship convinces the world that Jesus is God

The apostle John records one of the most fantastic prayers of history when Jesus makes an astonishing request to his Father; he asked for the unity of the Church, that his disciples be one, as he and the Father were one. Can you imagine that? Jesus is one with the Father!

The most extraordinary thing is the motive by which he made this request in prayer. He said:

> *That they all may be one, as You, Father, are in Me, and I in You; that they also may be one in Us, that the world may believe that You sent Me. I in them, and You in Me; that they may be made perfect in one, and that the world may know that You have sent Me, and have loved them as You have loved Me. (John 17:21, 23)*

The world will only believe in Jesus, if we live in the unity of fellowship. Christian unity wins more people to God than evangelism does. The truth is that Jesus said that the world would only recognize us as his disciples if we love one another (John 13:35). Fellowship is the means by which we express this love to the world.

We are members of one another

God has commanded us to serve one another.

> *As each one has received a gift, minister it to one another, as good stewards of the manifold grace of God. (1 Peter 4:10)*

The church is the dream that God has hidden in his heart since the beginning of time. You have the privilege of taking part in God's dream.

The word for fellowship in the original Greek is *Koinonia*. Its literal meaning is a shared life. Nobody possesses the fullness of God within himself. However, when we have fellowship, it is as if the divergent parts come together to form a unit, them the fullness of God can be manifested through it.

How can very large churches maintain true fellowship?

Fellowship is much more than just going to a church meeting and sitting next to a brother or sister whose name you may not even know. Spiritual fellowship unites all believers of all ages. This is fine, but we also need fellowship that involves communication.

We all need to share our life and feel part of a community by knowing others and allowing others to know us. Large churches can frighten some people at first. However, don't worry because when we meet in cells we can also be a very small church.

At the Sunday morning worship services you can have fellowship with the whole church, in the Spirit. However, during the week, in the cells, you can enjoy the life of the church, the fellowship of the brethren in a much more practical and intimate way.

Two types of meetings

In the Vine, we have two types of meetings: the celebration service, on Sundays, and the weekly cell group meeting usually on Wednesday evenings. At the celebration service, we teach the Word and minister to God as a Body. In the cell, we serve each other, allow others to know us, and get to know each other.

What is a cell group?

The cells are places of life. They are branches of the vine spread throughout the city. They are our manner of being the Church.

In a practical way, the cell is a group of 7 to 15 people that meet weekly to learn how to be a family, worship the Lord, build up each other's spiritual life, pray one for another and bring people to Christ.

Normally, each cell begins with at least seven people, but should never have more than fifteen members. When it reaches this limit, it should multiply into two new cells. Most likely, you are already participating in a cell group that will soon multiply and then you can see this marvelous process occur.

The objectives of cell groups

In a general way, the goal of the cell is to be the church in a practical way, ministering to one another. We can sum up its objectives in four points.

Fellowship - We grow in fellowship through the development of a shared life, common goals, and by affirming a mutual covenant among all members.

Teaching - We offer an atmosphere favorable to spiritual growth, practical learning and loving discipline.

Multiplication – The cell is where we spiritually feed, protect and supply the new brothers and sisters.

Service – In the cell, each member is a minister that exercises his or her gifts for mutual service.

Acts 2:42-47 paints a picture of that which we are seeking to accomplish in the cell groups:

- And they continued steadfastly in the apostles' doctrine
- And fellowship, in the breaking of bread,
- And in prayers
- Now all who believed were together, and had all things in common,
- And divided them among all, as anyone had need
- So continuing daily with one accord in the temple,
- And breaking bread from house to house, they ate their food with gladness and simplicity of heart,
- Praising God and having favor with all the people. And the Lord added to the church daily those who were being saved.

The cells are the way we express ourselves as a Church. We do not concern ourselves in doing different activities or putting on various programs. We concentrate our efforts on a single objective: building up strong cells that multiply themselves once per year.

Our church operates through the cells. Teaching, mutual care, sharing, love, encouragement, gifts, service, everything is done through the cells. After all, we are a church in cells.

Useful tips

The bible teaches many ways that we can have fellowship with the brethren. Practice them in your cell:

- Love the brethren

    A new commandment I give to you, that you love one another; as I have loved you, that you also love one another. (John 13:34)

- Welcome new converts

    Therefore receive one another, just as Christ also received us, to the glory of God. (Romans 15:7)

- Greet them whenever you see them

Greet one another with a kiss of love. Peace to you all who are in Christ Jesus. Amen. (1 Peter 5:14)

- Cooperate with the brethren

that there should be no schism in the body, but that the members should have the same care for one another. (1 Corinthians 12:25)

- Subject yourself to them

submitting to one another in the fear of God. (Ephesians 5:21)

- Don't judge anyone

Therefore let us not judge one another anymore, but rather resolve this, not to put a stumbling block or a cause to fall in our brother's way. (Romans 14:13)

- Don't gossip

Do not speak evil of one another, brethren. He who speaks evil of a brother and judges his brother, speaks evil of the law and judges the law. But if you judge the law, you are not a doer of the law but a judge. (James 4:11)

- Don't complain about others

Do not grumble against one another, brethren, lest you be condemned. Behold, the Judge is standing at the door! (James 5:9)

- Don't fight

But if you bite and devour one another, beware lest you be consumed by one another! (Galatians 5:15)

- Don't exalt yourself

Let us not become conceited, provoking one another, envying one another. (Galatians 5:26)

- Don't lie

Do not lie to one another, since you have put off the old man with his deeds, and have put on the new man who is renewed in knowledge according to the image of him who created him, (Colossians 3:9-10)

- Build up the brethren

  Therefore comfort each other and edify one another, just as you also are doing. (1 Thessalonians 5:11)

- Teach and counsel

  Let the word of Christ dwell in you richly in all wisdom, teaching and admonishing one another in psalms and hymns and spiritual songs, singing with grace in your hearts to the Lord. (Colossians 3:16)

- Exhort each other when you meet together

  but exhort one another daily, while it is called "Today," lest any of you be hardened through the deceitfulness of sin. (Hebrews 3:13)

- Serve the brethren

  For you, brethren, have been called to liberty; only do not use liberty as an opportunity for the flesh, but through love serve one another. (Galatians 5:13)

- Carry each other's burdens

  Bear one another's burdens, and so fulfill the law of Christ. (Galatians 6:2)

- Be hospitable

  Be hospitable to one another without grumbling. (1 Peter 4:9)

- Forgive those who offend you

  And be kind to one another, tenderhearted, forgiving one another, even as God in Christ forgave you. (Ephesians 4:32)

- Don't consider yourself holier than others

  Confess your trespasses to one another, and pray for one another, that you may be healed. The effective, fervent prayer of a righteous man avails much. (James 5:16)

- Support the weak

We then who are strong ought to bear with the scruples of the weak, and not to please ourselves. (Romans 15:1)

- Please the brethren

Let each of us please his neighbor for his good, leading to edification. For even Christ did not please himself; but as it is written, "The reproaches of those who reproached You fell on Me." (Romans 15:2, 3)

- Suffer loss

Now therefore, it is already an utter failure for you that you go to law against one another. Why do you not rather accept wrong? Why do you not rather let yourselves be cheated? (1 Corinthians 6:7)

- Consider others superior to yourself

Therefore if there is any consolation in Christ, if any comfort of love, if any fellowship of the Spirit, if any affection and mercy, fulfill my joy by being like-minded, having the same love, being of one accord, of one mind. Let nothing be done through selfish ambition or conceit, but in lowliness of mind let each esteem others better than himself. (Philippians 2:1-3)

APPENDIX

CONFESSIONS OF THE WORD

Here are some biblical confessions that you can use to build up your faith. Practice them during the twelve weeks of this series of studies. Remember what Jesus said in Romans 10:10: For with the heart one believes unto righteousness, and with the mouth confession is made unto salvation.

PSALM 23

The Lord is my shepherd I shall not want (Psalm 23:1). The phrase "I shall not want" means "I will never lack or be without", therefore:

I will never lack peace (Ephesians 2:14)

I will never lack health (Exodus 15:26)

I will never lack provision (Philippians 4:19)

I will never lack prosperity (Psalm 1:3)

I will never lack guidance (Psalm 35:23)

I will never lack strength (2 Chronicles 10:4)

I will never lack power (Philippians 4:13)

You make me to lie down in green pastures; You are my spiritual food (John 6:48). You are the bread of life upon which I feed every second in my spirit.

You make me to lie down and you are my rest (Hebrews 4:3). You lead me beside the still waters. You are the living water that quenches my thirst (John 4:10-14). You draw me near to you. My heart is thirsty for your presence.

You restore my soul. You restore and heal me, because Jesus took all of my infirmities to the cross (Isaiah 53:5-6). You have taken upon yourself all of my infirmities.

You lead me in the paths of righteousness for your name's sake.

Therefore, I believe that there will always be a voice with me saying, "This is the way follow it" (Isaiah 30:21)

Yea, though I walk through the valley of the shadow of death, I will fear no evil for You are with me. You will never under any circumstances leave me or abandon me (Hebrews 13:5)

I believe that your goodness and mercy shall follow me all the days of my life; and I will dwell in your house forever. (Psalm 23:6)

THE POWER OF GOD

Yours, O LORD, is the greatness, The power and the glory, The victory and the majesty; For all that is in heaven and in earth is Yours; Yours is the kingdom, O LORD, And You are exalted as head over all. Both riches and honor come from You, And You reign over all. In your hand is power and might; In Your hand is the power to make great and to give strength to all. (1 Chronicles 29:12) I know that You can do everything, and that no one can withhold Your purposes from You. (Job 42:2).

When Abram was ninety-nine years old, the LORD appeared to him and said, *"I am Almighty God; walk before Me and be blameless."* (Genesis 17:1) Is anything too hard for the LORD? (Genesis 18:14) Who has measured the waters in the hollow of his hand, Measured heaven with a span and calculated the dust of the earth in a measure? (Isaiah 40:12)

Lift up your eyes on high, and see who has created these things, Who brings out their host by number; he calls them all by name, By the greatness of his might And the strength of his power (Isaiah 40:26). There is nothing too hard for You (Jeremiah 32:17). I work, and who will reverse it? (Isaiah 43:13). If you open, no one closes; if you close, no one opens. All things are possible with you.

You can raise up the invalid, give sight to the blind and renew the strength of the downcast.

You cause the sterile woman to become a mother of many children. You heal my infirmities and fill me with abundance of prosperity.

You cause the lame to leap like a deer, and the tongue of the dumb to sing.

You have the power to transform the alcoholic, the drug addict and criminal with the breath of your mouth. You raise up the miserable and unworthy making them worthy and prosperous and transform the homosexual and the prostitute.

You can resurrect the dead from the grave, strengthen the weary, and sustain the weak.

You are able to do exceedingly abundantly above all that we ask or think, according to the power that works in us (Ephesians 3:20). I quiet my soul because I know that You are the all-powerful and omnipotent God, the great El Shaddai.

I AM A NEW CREATURE

> *Therefore, if anyone is in Christ, he is a new creation; old things have passed away; behold, all things have become new. (2 Corinthians 5:17)*

I am in Christ Jesus! I am a new Creature in Christ! I have been re-created! The life and nature of God are within me. I have passed from death to life! I am a new creature!

> *But as many as received him, to them he gave the right to become children of God, to those who believe in his name: who were born, not of blood, nor of the will of the flesh, nor of the will of man, but of God. (John 1:12, 13)*

I have received power to become a son of God because I have been born of his will. I am part of his family. God is my Father! He loves me, and provides for my needs and takes care of me.

> *having been born again, not of corruptible seed but incorruptible, through the word of God which lives and abides forever, (1 Peter 1:23)*

I am begotten of God. I am born of God, of incorruptible seed, by the living Word of God. I have been born in the spiritual dimension, and I have received eternal life and have become a branch of the Vine by the unchangeable Word of God.

> *For we are his workmanship, created in Christ Jesus for good works, which God prepared beforehand that we should walk in them. (Ephesians 2:10)*

I am the workmanship of God. He has made me a new creature. He created me in Christ Jesus for good works. I see myself as God sees me; therefore, I reject all complexes and timidity. I see myself in Christ Jesus.

For you were bought at a price; therefore glorify God in your body and in your spirit, which are God's. (1 Corinthians 6:20)

I have been bought with a high price, obtained and paid for in order to be exclusively His. Never again will I say that I am worthless, since my worth is the price that he paid to redeem me, the price of the blood of Jesus. I no longer belong to myself; I belong to the Lord Jesus.

I AM FREE FROM SIN

I am free indeed because the Son has set me free (John 8:36). How can I remain in sin since I have died to it? (Romans 6:2). Because my old man was crucified with him, that the body of sin might be done away with, that I should no longer be a slave of sin (Romans 6:6). Therefore I reckon myself to be dead indeed to sin, but alive to God in Christ Jesus my Lord (Romans 6:11), for sin shall not have dominion over me, for I am not under law but under grace (Romans 6:14).

Previously I was a slave to sin, but now having been freed from sin, I have become a servant of righteousness, a servant of God, and have become a slave of God, and have fruit to holiness (Romans 6:21)

The law of the Spirit of life in Christ Jesus has made me free from the law of sin and death (Romans 8:2). I have been born of God, therefore I cannot continue in the practice of sin (1 John 3:8, 9). Also I overcome the world, because whoever is born of God does not sin; but he who has been born of God keeps himself, and the wicked one does not touch him (1 John 5:18).

FAITH IS THE VICTORY

For whatever is born of God overcomes the world. This is the victory that has overcome the world: our faith (1 John 5:4). Although I am in the world, I do not belong to the world. I am of God and he who is in me is greater than he who is in the world (1 John 4:4).

The devil is in the world. However, God is greater and gives me the victory over all battles against the enemy. The Lord always leads us in triumph in Christ (2 Corinthians 2:14). For this purpose, the Son of

God was manifested, that he might destroy the works of the devil (1 John 3:8). I overcome the world by faith and destroy the works of the Devil, because I am a son of God.

Sin is in the world. However, he that is in me is greater than sin and leads me to victory. Christ Jesus has already overcome sin and by faith, I am now alive in this victory.

I overcome the world with its passions, sicknesses and afflictions. If I cannot pass over the affliction, I will go around it, if I cannot go around it, I will pass under it. If I cannot pass under it, I will pass through it, because greater is he that is in me than he that is in the world (1 John 4:4) I am born of God, and by releasing my faith through the words of my mouth, I overcome the world.

The just shall live by his faith (Romans 1:17) I live by faith in the living Word of God. I act upon the truth of the Word. All of my words are words of faith. I reject words of despair, doubt, unbelief and fear because with the heart one believes and with the mouth confession is made unto salvation (Romans 10:10). I believe on God's Word with my heart and confess with my mouth its promises and provisions. I am everything that God says I am and have everything that he says I have.

I fight the good fight of faith (1 Timothy 6:12). Faith comes by hearing God's Word and I decide to hear it more and more. I will have Bible revelation and my faith will continue to grow day by day.

By faith I speak in new tongues, cast out demons and heal sicknesses (Mark 16:17). By faith I undo the works of the devil, and call into existence the promises of God, subdue the devil, practice righteousness and shut the mouths of lions (Hebrews 11:33). Faith is taking what God's Word says seriously and putting it into practice. I live by faith and practice the Word.

VICTORY OVER THE ENEMY

Nor give place to the devil. (Ephesians 4:27)

I give no place to the enemy. I do not give him the slightest opportunity. As a watchman of God's property, which is my body, I permit no invaders. I give neither place nor support to the devil. I provide no foothold of sin or worldliness. The devil has nothing in me.

And they overcame him by the blood of the Lamb and by

the word of their testimony, and they did not love their lives
to the death. (Revelation 12:11)

I am an overcomer. By the blood of the Lamb and the word of our testimony, I overcome the devil in all confrontations. I cease not to speak, but constantly proclaim God's Word, which is the sword of the Spirit that penetrates and destroys the works of the devil.

Which he worked in Christ when he raised him from the
dead and seated him at his right hand in the heavenly
places, far above all principality and power and might and
dominion, and every name that is named, not only in this
age but also in that which is to come. And he put all things
under his feet, and gave him to be head over all things to
the church, which is his body, the fullness of him who fills
all in all. (Ephesians 1:20-23)

God placed Christ above everything and everyone. All things are underneath his feet.

For more information about other titles visit:
http://www.amazon.com/Richard-Lee-Spinos/e/B00A911TZK
FB: Why be Holy if Salvation is by Grace?
https://www.facebook.com/why.be.holy
Our church Facebook page -
http://www.facebook.com/TheVineFlorida
Our church websites - http://www.thevineusa.org/
http://www.thevineusa.com
The Vinebrancher blog - http://vinebrancher.com

Printed in Great Britain
by Amazon

61528372R00071